What People Are Say
The 10-Step Empowerment Series

"Through the use of introspective questions, the book invites the reader to take a journey of self-examination in order to accept the loss and to reengage in life."

—Ian Landry, MA, MSW, Case Manager

"Bevan has real-life experience in the area of loss and 'rebuilding' her life and self-esteem in the face of traumatic experiences such as being abandoned by a partner."

—Margaret M. Mustelier, Psy.D.

"Nowadays, there are too many books about adult loving relationships, but they usually are generic and abstract descriptions. This book is different because it moves to specificity and provides concrete steps to overcome a disrupting episode in our lives."

—Carlos J. Sanchez, MA, Family Therapist

"Lynda Bevan delivers what she promises in the title of the book: it is a practical guide and a no-nonsense approach. Her descriptions of the experiences are palpable."

—Chin Tao, LMFT

"This is a well thought out, useful little book that is an excellent guide for those recovering from a broken long-term relationship." —Robert Rich, MSc, PhD, M.A.P.S.,

"The book is studded with illuminating case studies and provides an excellent exposition of issues such as post-traumatic emotional responses, pre-trauma expectations, setting boundaries, forgiveness and acceptance, and the do's and don'ts of moving forward. A gem."

—Sam Vaknin, PhD
author *Malignant Self Love: Narcissism Revisited*

"Bevan provides practical steps to help a person begin the process of change, and during that process, to decide how the relationship will be affected, and whether to stay in the relationship, based on how your partner reacts to your new behaviors."

— Tyler R. Tichelaar, PhD
Author of *The Marquette Trilogy*

"This easy to relate to, solution-focused guide does not attempt to push an agenda; it simply provides a foundation of understanding along with the tools necessary to begin trusting one's own feelings again.. Bevan dedicates great thought towards realistic problem solving approaches while maintaining a focus on safety, health, and growth."

— Erin M. Hudges, LCSW
Rebecca's Reads

"I truly feel that every individual who is dealing with issues of some form of jealousy will greatly benefit from reading *Life Without Jealousy* by Lynda Bevan. This includes people who are not jealous themselves but are being affected by others who are. Learning to understand it, overcome it, and gain effective new ways to communicate will greatly improve the quality of our lives."

Paige Lovitt
— *Reader Views*

"

Life Without Jealousy

A Practical Guide

LYNDA BEVAN

THE 10-STEP EMPOWERMENT SERIES

Life Without Jealousy: A Practical Guide
Book #4 in the 10-Step Empowerment Series
Copyright © 2009, 2010 by Lynda Bevan

2nd Printing: January 2010

Library of Congress Cataloging-in-Publication Data

Bevan, Lynda.
  Life without jealousy : a practical guide / Lynda Bevan.
      p. cm. -- (10-step empowerment series ; 4)
  Includes bibliographical references and index.
  ISBN-13: 978-1-932690-85-9 (trade paper : alk. paper)
  ISBN-10: 1-932690-85-9 (trade paper : alk. paper)
  ISBN-13: 978-1-61599-023-8 (hardcover: alk. paper)
  ISBN-10: 1-61599-023-2 (hardcover: alk. paper)

  1. Jealousy. I. Title.
  BF575.J4B48 2009
  152.4'8--dc22

                                        2009000115

Distributed by: Ingram Book Group, New Leaf Distributing,
Quality Books.

Published by:
Loving Healing Press
5145 Pontiac Trail
Ann Arbor, MI 48105-9627

info@LHPress.com   www.LovingHealing.com
Tollfree 888-761-6268   Fax 734-663-6861

THE 10-STEP EMPOWERMENT SERIES

- Life After Your Lover Walks Out (2006)
- Life After Betrayal (2007)
- Stop Being Pushed Around! (2008)
- Life Without Jealousy (2009)

About our Series Editor, Robert Rich, Ph.D.

Loving Healing Press is pleased to announce Robert Rich, Ph.D. as Series Editor for the *10-Step Empowerment Series*. This exciting new series conveys practical guides written by seasoned therapists for solving real-life problems.

Robert Rich, M.Sc., Ph.D., M.A.P.S., A.A.S.H. is a highly experienced counseling psychologist. His website www.anxietyanddepression-help.com is a storehouse of helpful information for people suffering from anxiety and depression.

Bob is also a multiple award-winning writer of both fiction and non-fiction, and a professional editor. His writing is displayed at www.bobswriting.com. You are advised not to visit him there unless you have the time to get lost for a while.

Three of his books are tools for psychological self-help: *Anger and Anxiety: Be in charge of your emotions and control phobias*, *Personally Speaking: Single session email therapy*, and *Cancer: A personal challenge*. However, his philosophy and psychological knowledge come through in all his writing, which is perhaps why three of his books have won international awards, and he has won many minor prizes. Dr. Rich currently resides at Wombat Hollow in Australia.

Contents

1 | What is Jealousy?

The focus of this book is to understand and recover from the emotion of jealousy within a relationship/marriage/partnership. Step 1 will concentrate on jealousy. Step 2 will concentrate on Envy. In Step 3, I will attempt to explain each type of jealousy before moving on to the thoughts, feelings, speech, and action that take place when jealousy is present in your relationship.

Jealousy is typically used to describe the thought, feeling, and behavior that occur when a person believes a valued relationship is being threatened by a rival. Jealousy is a destructive emotion, hell-bent on causing unhappiness. It can strike at any moment, eroding your mind and heart with thoughts and feelings that are meant to be emotionally destructive. Jealousy cunningly lies under the surface of love, hate, and desire, waiting for the opportunity to jump out and show itself. Jealousy takes pleasure in sowing seeds of discontentment in your mind and is only sated when disharmony occurs.

All of us have experienced jealousy of some description. I believe jealousy is the result of a creative overactive imagination. If you have a seed of doubt in your mind about your partner and/or your relationship, your jealous thoughts will take you through a series of negative scenarios as a means of torturing you. It feels terrible but you, somehow, can't stop or help yourself from sliding down the road to despair. Jealousy brings about an emotional state of being "out of control." Only someone who has experienced jealousy can fully comprehend how awful this feeling is. You know what you are doing but you can't stop it. Jealousy feeds you the mental images of your worst scenario and leaves you feeling angry, empty, and dissatisfied. Being jealous says a lot about who you are.

Fear Feeds Jealousy

You are afraid of...
- Your partner leaving you;
- Being betrayed;
- Losing face;
- Having "egg on your face" (being humiliated);
- Losing your self-esteem;
- Hurting your self-confidence;
- Your appearance not being good enough to attract a partner;
- Weighing too much to be attractive;
- Being embarrassed by your lack of skills;
- Not being good enough;
- Being an inadequate lover;
- Being unable to sustain a relationship;
- Communicating about this with family, friends, and/or partners.

Each of us has a unique list of our own. Write out your own list and discover your own problem areas with regard to jealousy.

Where Did the Seed of Doubt Arise?

- Have you always been jealous?
- Were you jealous as a child?
- Were you loved as a child?
- Is one or both of your parents jealous?
- Has a past partner alerted you to jealousy by betraying you?
- Are your family or friends jealous of you?

Make a list of all the times you have been jealous. State what it was you were jealous of. Are you still jealous of those things you have identified? Do you believe you are unworthy of having a partner?

Wherever and whenever the seed of jealousy was planted, it is now firmly positioned in your mind. Jealousy is an indicator that you place no value on yourself. It searches in your memory for examples and scripts that prove you have a right to be jealous. Your mind is like a computer that forages through your mental files to find evidence that you are unworthy, and that it is only a question of time before your partner moves on to someone much better than you believe you are.

How Can I Accept Myself?

The first step in overcoming jealousy is to learn to accept and love yourself for the person you are.

You can do this by listening to...

- What you are feeling;
- What you are thinking;
- What you are saying;
- The negative stuff that you say about yourself (mind chatter);
- The old pattern of thoughts regurgitating and repeating yet again.

In order to rid yourself of jealous thoughts, you must clear your mind of stuff (old habits and beliefs) you have been holding on to. Erase the repeating thoughts that are the root cause of you inflicting this negative pain on yourself.

You can do this by...

- Writing your negative thoughts down on a notepad;

- Changing the negative thought script that you have identified to a positive thought script. If you write these positive thoughts down, they will form a definite script in your mind;
- Repeating these positive script changes you have made, over and over again. This exercise will help to reduce, and eventually rid you of, your negative beliefs;
- Remembering "I am what I think I am;"
- Remembering "Others are what I tell myself they are;"
- Using your energy to create the person you want to be;
- Understanding that you must take responsibility for creating your emotional security. Don't look to your partner to provide you with emotional safety.

I can assure you that if you do this exercise and stick with it, you will see the benefits in a very short time.

Ask yourself: Am I...

- Suspicious of my partner?
- Frequently checking up on my partner?
- Searching through my partner's jacket pockets or reading his/her mobile phone messages?
- Constantly questioning my partner about where s/he is going or what s/he is doing?
- Withdrawing from my partner without giving an explanation as to why I am doing this?
- Suspicious when I meet new people?
- Frightened of change?
- Frightened of being abandoned?

If you answered "yes" to most of the above, then you have selected the right book to help you overcome this problem.

Take time out to look at each negative script you have identified.

Looking back from now, ask yourself...

- Have I ever had any cause to be suspicious or jealous of my partner?
- Has this cause ever created a rift between me and my partner?
- Do I think I handled the situation in the right way?
- Can I see that my negative thoughts produced negative results?
- Do I think I behaved reasonably?
- Do I believe I acted in a rational manner?
- Do I think I exaggerated the situation?
- Would I handle the situation differently in hindsight?
- Am I focusing on my partner because I am unable to focus on myself?
- Do I trust my intuition?
- Do I trust my perception?
- Do I trust myself?

All these questions are important in order for you to see clearly, on reflection, that you may have made a "mountain out of a molehill" through your own fears and emotional insecurity. These issues, which are seated in the past, stem either from your childhood or from your recent adult relationships. This results in you feeling out-of-control and unable to sustain a healthy relationship. Before you can have a better relationship with your partner, you must exorcise these irrational fears. Get rid of them, once and for all. Take a peek at your past history, alone or with a friend or therapist, and you will discover how this negativity came about.

Once you have identified the root cause, don't make the mistake of hanging on to it, thereby justifying your present behavior. Look at it, accept it, and decide to "move on" from it. Is there any benefit from reliving your past *ad infinitum*?

Sufficient to say that you have allocated the cause, and are now ready to address it. By doing these exercises, you will find it easier to let go of your destructive negative jealous feelings and embrace new positive thoughts, feelings, and attitude.

Jealousy is powerful and dangerous, and is a real issue. It destroys your relationships and it destroys you in the process. It is one of the biggest emotional problems and is a barrier to creating a successful partnership. You feel jealous when you think that your partner is being unfaithful or looking at someone for too long. You see other people as "predators" who are trying to take your partner away from you. When this happens, you feel physically sick, with your heart pounding and on the verge of a full-blown panic attack. Jealousy isolates you. However, the good news is that jealousy can be controlled. It will not go away forever. It will lurk in the depths of your mind, ready and waiting to erupt if you allow it. It needs to be put away into a safe place with you holding the key. You are in control.

Take into consideration the following suggestions:

- Do not rely on your partner to make your life complete;
- Create your life and fill it with stuff you want to do;
- Have mutual friends but also have your own circle of friends;
- Value who you are;
- Learn to be more understanding;
- Learn to be more honest;
- Learn to be more trusting.

The next step is to learn to have faith: faith in yourself, and faith in your partner.

What Is Faith?

Faith is blind. Faith is a strong belief. It's a feeling of warmth and loyalty you generate when you believe in yourself, your partner, your family, or others. Without having faith in your relationship, you will flounder and fall by the wayside into an emotional, unhealthy abyss. A healthy relationship is based on trust and faith. Decide together to be open with each other. Communicate your worst fears to each other and work through these fears to a positive outcome.

> "Jealousy, the jaundice of the soul."
>   John Dryden (1631-1700)

2 | What is Envy?

How does envy differ from jealousy in a relationship?

- Jealousy supports the fact that you want to keep what you have. It is a righteous indignation that "what's yours" stays that way.

- Envy is the desire to own something that is not yours.

- Envy can be seen as a mild jealousy which can be a route to improved capabilities. The term used for this is "creative envy." It is part of a process to improve by putting pressure on yourself to develop new skills.

Some suggest that the main difference between these two words is the involvement of a *third party*. The jealous person wants all the attention to be on them, but a third party in this equation would rob them of this attention. The third party is seen as a predator and a rival, and the jealous person will be very unhappy if the person they are jealous of gives any attention to the third party.

Another common distinction between jealousy and envy is that envy is the desire for something *in general* (more money), whereas jealousy is the desire to have something *in particular*, and to take it from someone else (one is jealous of a friend's girlfriend/boyfriend).

Envy begrudges another person's success, possessions, and lifestyle, even if they earned it by their own hard work. You may remember that the seven deadly sins are anger, covetousness, envy, gluttony, lust, pride, and sloth. Envy is the age-old monster that motivated Cain to murder his brother Abel. According to the Bible, it's an evil that leads to quarrels, fights, disorder, and "every vile practice."

> "But if ye have bitter envying and strife in your hearts, glory not, and lie not against the truth."
>
> James 3:14 (KJV)

Envy Rots the Soul

When you see something or somebody having what you yearn for, the envy you feel squeezes the very life out of your being. It highlights the dissatisfaction that you believe that you haven't got what you want in your life. This can happen at any place and time. Envy holds no boundaries, but strikes with a powerful force. Envy is one of the deadly sins and is named such because it can cause serious emotional and physical damage to yourself and others. It acts like a cancer, eating away at the very core of your being.

As Proverbs says, "A tranquil heart gives life to the flesh, but envy makes the bones rot" (Prov. 14:30, ESV). When envy strikes, it takes away your logical, lateral thinking pattern and instead you become irrational, unreasonable, paranoid, and out of control; and you display warped thinking. Shakespeare called it "the green-eyed monster." Envy destroys relationships. What does envy do to you; how is it displayed?

Here are some examples of what you may become...

- Spiteful
- Resentful
- Obsessive
- Competitive
- Arrogant
- Paranoid
- Unhappy
- Distrustful
- Dissatisfied
- Driven
- Slanderous
- Malicious
- Gossipy
- Poisonous

Make your own list. Envy is the rust in any relationship. It creeps around your thoughts and corrodes your emotional intelligence. You can't get away from it as it strangles your feelings, attitude, and behavior.

The English word *envy* is from the Latin word *invidia*, meaning "to look with ill-will or malicious intent" at another person. It is close in meaning to the words *resent, begrudge.*

How do you rid yourself of envy?

First of all, by owning that you are envious! Do this simple exercise:

1. Write down exactly you are envious of. Is it people, possessions, professions, relationships, money, behavior, etc.?

2. Continue this exercise, and write down opposite each item that you have found that you envy, how you can change your belief and reaction to those issues.

Use the form on the following page to do this, or write in your own private journal.

What am I envious of?	How can I change my belief or reaction?

I want you to answer each of the following questions with a Yes or No. Take some time with this exercise. It is important that you are clear and honest in your observations of yourself.

Ask yourself...

- Are they spiteful to me? (people or their individual successes);
- Are they ignoring me? (people or their individual successes);
- Do they put me down? (people or their individual successes);
- Do they make me feel inferior? (people or their individual successes).

Let's take this a step further.

What has your partner said and/or done to you to make you envious?

These are some suggestions to help you unravel and uncover your thoughts and feelings:

Ask yourself...

- Has my partner called me names?
- Has my partner left me out of a girls'/boys' night out?
- Do people or my partner poke fun at me?
- Have I overheard some gossip about myself?
- How can I be successful in my chosen career?
- How can I be positive and proactive?

Dig deep beneath your feelings and unearth exactly what makes you envious of these people. Take each question and explain exactly what you think and believe. When you have finished writing down your answers to each of the questions, I want you to imagine yourself sharing this information with a close friend.

How would you feel sharing this information...?

- Justified?
- Stubborn?
- Frustrated?
- Guilty?
- Embarrassed?

- Ashamed?
- Secretive?
- Unburdened?
- Relieved?

Most people, who undertake this exercise, find that they have difficulty identifying exactly what they are envious of. If you are one of these people, this exercise will unearth these issues and you will see that you have no reason to continue to feel envious of these people or situations. If, however, you still feel envious, then you will need to take this exercise one step further.

You can do this by...

- Confronting the people you have identified that you are jealous of, and be prepared to discuss your issues with that person;
- Confronting this person without being aggressive;
- Confronting each person individually;
- Being prepared to be open, and to listen to what each of them are saying to you;
- Being prepared to explain to each of them that you have heard that they are talking about you behind your back and that this situation is making you unhappy;
- Being prepared to ask them "What don't you like about me?"

Confronting your innermost fears and thoughts will assist you in overcoming the problem. In some cases, your worst fear might be justified. However, when you do this exercise, you are most often left feeling a bit silly that you have been thinking in this way. If this is the case, then you will see that the problem is not with those other people—but with you.

You should then look into your mental thought patterns and attitudes and do the necessary readjustments. In other words, you need to repent (change your mind). Turn your negative thought processes that are displaying envy and change them to a more positive emotion. Remember: treat others as you would like others to treat you.

If you needed to do the last exercise and now understand that you had no cause for feeling envious, you might like to:

- Send them a card, thanking them for listening and putting your mind at rest;
- Ask each person in turn around to your home for coffee.

> "Love does not envy"
>
> (1 Corinthians 13:4)

Grudges

Grudges are the things we remember and hold on to with bitterness, anger, resentment, and/or hostility. If you are holding on to a grudge, you are ensuring that you remain a miserable victim. Holding on to a grudge causes more harm to you than to the person you are holding the grudge against. It makes you unhappy. It stops you from achieving personal development, and it is disempowering. In order to move on from a grudge, you must **forgive** the other person for whatever you believe they have done to you.

Dr. Phil McGraw quotes studies that show feelings of grudge increase stress, raise blood pressure, promote ulcers, and a multitude of other side effects. In short, it can ruin your health and shorten your life.

A grudge is a tool to gain control over someone who, you believe, has wronged you.

A study at Michigan State University found that 48 percent of us admit to holding grudges, and that probably the actual figure is much higher than that.

Ask yourself…

- Do I hold grudges?
- Do I repeat the cause of the grudge over and over again?
- Is this grudge affecting my life?
- Do I find it easy to forgive?
- When I am hurt, what does it take from the other person before I am willing to reconcile?
- Do I build a wall of silence?
- Do I withdraw into myself?
- Do I persecute my victim?
- Do I persecute myself?

Bringing the past into the present and holding on to a grudge will cause irreparable damage to a relationship. Ask yourself, "Would I like someone to be constantly reminding me of a mistake or misdeed from my past?" It will stir old wounds and create a distance between you and your partner/friend/family member, etc. You have probably punished this person many times over the years (secretly or overtly).

Ask yourself, "If the same circumstances were repeated today, would my partner/friend/family member still react in the way that has hurt me so much?" If the answer is "no," and you can see that this person has grown up and made positive changes to themselves, then you are doing this person/these people and yourself a great disservice hanging on the grudge.

The grudge you are holding onto is from the past and should be left there. Take the grudge out of your memory, examine it for the last time, and then put it in the trash can that is stored in a part of your thought processes. The past is important so that we can "learn from it and not relive it."

> "To forgive is to overcome."
> Jeffrie G. Murphy, *Getting Even*

Forgiveness enables you to...

- Make a conscious choice and a decision;
- Retain your power (it's hard to come by, so don't waste it);
- Retain your energy (it's hard to come by, so don't waste it);
- Let go of hurt (angry is how you behave when you are hurt);
- Let go of pain;
- Banish negative thoughts;
- Release your anger.

When you hold grudges against someone, you are using up/draining all your power and energy in a negative way. It takes a lot of energy and power to hold on to outdated grudges. It is a waste of the essential power and energy that you need to live your life in a positive way. It's pointless holding on to the things of the past. You can't change the things that have happened to you in your life, but you have control and can decide how you think, feel, and respond to them now.

We all talk to ourselves all of the time. It's an unconscious act. Be aware of your inner dialogue (mind chatter). Remember it and write it down. You will be surprised and amazed at the things that you tell yourself that are both negative and useless. After you have written down your thoughts, concentrate on changing the words from negative to positive, from reactive to proactive, from inappropriate to appropriate, from impertinent to pertinent. This is the first step to an emotional closure on your past negative memories and associated mind chatter.

Ask yourself about this person...

- Has the grudge stopped me seeing someone in my life?
- Is my relationship to that person important to me?
- Do I want to spend the rest of my life playing the injured victim?
- Am I storing up more grudges against that person, or others?

Answer the above questions honestly. Be brutal with yourself. Get to the very core of your inner belief in respect of the grudge (or grudges).

Ask yourself about this grudge...

- Why do I need to hold on to the grudge?
- Is it to teach that person a lesson?
- Is it to let someone stew in their own juices?
- Is it because I don't think that I should make the first move in putting it right?
- Is it because I believe that even if that person says sorry, I still wouldn't be able to forgive them?

You actually have a choice with most things in life. Remember that *you* are choosing to hold on to the grudge. You are the one who is replaying the scene over and over again and hurting yourself in the process. Make a choice to get over it. Let it go. Move on. You can let go of anger and hurt; you just need to make the decision to do so.

The "blame culture trail" is a road to nowhere. Stop playing this game. Take the first step and approach whoever it is that you are holding the grudge against. Confronting your issue in this way will empower you and you will regain your confidence and self-respect. Be prepared to calmly talk through this issue with this person and, if need be, be prepared to say "sorry." Ask yourself, is "sorry" such a difficult word to say? Learning to **forgive** is not an easy task to undertake. First of all, you need to forgive yourself and you will be better placed to forgive others. When you forgive someone, you are freeing them and yourself from the prison the grudge has created within you.

> "Be kind and compassionate to one another, forgive each other."
>
> Paul's instruction given in Ephesians 4:32

Suspicion (doubt, mistrust)

If you are suspicious of some people, or of your partner, then you are leading a worrying, miserable, emotionally draining life. You are frustrated and exhausted with this continual nagging that persists in your mind.

Who are you suspicious of?
- My work colleagues?
- My family?
- My friends?
- My partner?
- Myself? (Turning your suspicion inward and being afraid to be found out about something).

Write the answers down after carefully thinking about them.

What can you do to stop this vicious circle of mistrust?

Ask yourself these questions:
- Do I believe I am a popular person?
- Do I have many friends?
- Do I believe I am close to my family?
- Do I believe I can confide in my family?
- Do I believe I know when I started being suspicious?
- Do I know exactly what I am suspicious of?

It is very important that you answer each of these questions. Write them down and take your time. Really think about the answers. They will reflect who you are. From these answers you can decide that perhaps you need more suitable or positive friends or maybe that you would like to be closer to your family. If you believe you are suffering from depression, these questions will be difficult to answer positively.

The whole point of these exercises is for you to learn more about yourself, to find out:

- What you like;
- What you don't like;
- Who you like;
- Who you don't like;
- If you have changed in attitude;
- If you are secretive;
- If you are you putting on an act when you are with friends and family.

You might be surprised with your assessment of yourself and your life, and this will help you make adjustments as appropriate.

Here are some questions to help you cope with the nagging suspicion that your partner is having an affair:

Ask yourself: Do you believe…

- Your partner is fully committed to your relationship?
- If your partner was unhappy, s/he would share these feelings with you?
- You can trust your partner?
- You are jealous of your partner?
- You were jealous in a previous relationship?
- Your partner ever gave you reason to mistrust him/her?

Answer these questions as honestly as possible. It is vital that you see past the words on the paper and are able to link into your intuitive and perceptive skills. Don't be of the mindset that screams, "I never expect anyone to be faithful to me!" or "I am unworthy of having a committed relationship." A healthy relationship between two people should be able to handle these issues that are mentally and emotionally destroying you.

If you haven't done so already, try discussing your concerns and fears with your partner. Don't accuse. Be realistic, reasonable, and listen to what your partner is saying to you. If you don't understand something that is said, ask for clarification. Make sure that you understand the issue from your partner's perspective. If you are able to discuss all your fears and suspicions with your partner, it will avoid the inevitable "spying" game that comes with the territory of suspicion:

Ask yourself: Are you...?

- Checking your partner's cell phone?
- Checking your partner's pockets?
- Writing down the mileage odometer of his/her car?
- Following your partner?
- Logging into your partner's e-mails?
- Reading and checking bank statements for gotchas?
- Reading and checking phone bills?
- Checking credit card statements?
- Searching your partner's study and/or briefcase?

Doing all these things is demoralizing for you. So, decide not to do it anymore. Instead, tell your partner what things you cannot and will not tolerate.

Here are some suggestions: Make it clear that...

- You won't share your partner with anyone else;
- You won't put up with secret meetings;

- You don't want to be with someone who lies to you;
- You want to be able to contact your partner at any time via the cell phone;
- You want to be the top priority (everyone else comes after you);
- You want your partner to be able to share problems and worries with you. Whether the problem is work or your relationship, you need to know from your partner as this will stop you second-guessing and maybe getting it wrong.

If you have completed the questions and answers, you will feel less insecure and more confident. Make a conscious effort to stop being distrustful, pathetic, weak, and dependent. Own who you are and be proud of your efforts to change your attitude and behavior. If, however, you have found these exercises too difficult, perhaps you would consider the help of a counselor or therapist who will be trained to assist you with these issues.

> "Envy can be a positive motivator. Let it inspire you to work harder for what you want."
>
> Robert_Bringle

3 | Identifying Types of Jealousy

As stated in Step 1, below are many types of jealousy. I will explain each of them, before focusing on jealousy within a relationship/marriage/partnership.

- Sexual Jealousy
- Romantic Jealousy
- Possessive Jealousy
- Emotional Jealousy
- Marital Jealousy
- Financial Jealousy
- Material Jealousy
- Jealous of partner's relationship with children
- Work-related Jealousy
- Sibling Jealousy
- Violent Jealousy
- Pathological/Morbid Jealousy/Insane Jealousy

Jealousy is a complex emotion. It can be expressed in many different ways, as identified above. Sometimes, it is extremely difficult to see that someone is jealous, since it comes in so many varied guises.

Sexual Jealousy

Jealousy is rooted in insecurity. Put simply, it means that the person who is jealous is emotionally insecure within themselves and in their relationship with their partner. Feelings of jealousy arise from the belief that something in their life is causing them to be uncertain of their situation and future. In some cases, this belief and feeling is unfounded, and if this is so, then the jealous person needs to "find out" why they are feeling this raw emotion and address it, in order to remove this negativity that destroys relationships. This process is best achieved by engaging with a therapist / coun-

selor trained to unearth and identify issues from the past that
have contributed to the insecurity and the resulting jealousy.

Sexual Jealousy arises when one partner believes that their
partner is cheating on them or that their partner is giving a
third party more attention than they are receiving. It also occurs if the jealous person believes that the trust in the
partnership has been broken. Jealousy is a signal that something needs fixing.

**If you are the jealous person, ask yourself the following
questions: Does your jealousy...?**

- Cause arguments?
- Cause violence?
- Make your partner afraid of you?
- Allow you to control your partner's life?

Answer these questions honestly. Write your answers
down. If you suspect your partner has sexual feelings for
another person, then by writing your feelings down on paper,
you will be more able to see that either you have no reason
for your belief, or that you have just cause to believe that
your partner is thinking of another person or, worse, actually
having a sexual relationship with someone else.

The next step is to write down the evidence you have ac-
quired to substantiate your belief. Take your time with this
exercise. It is important that you write down all the experiences that have made you believe you have reason to be
jealous of your partner.

> "O beware, my lord, of jealousy; It is the green
> eyed monster which doth mock the meat it feeds on."
>   Shakespeare's *Othello*

Evidence to look for:

- Phone calls logged on your partner's cell phone;

- Phone bills and statements;
- Financial bank statements;
- Hidden statements;
- Your partner has become preoccupied with his/her appearance;
- Your partner is shaping up and losing weight;
- A change of hairstyle;
- A change in their fashion, i.e. new, trendier clothes;
- Your partner working late at the office;
- Your partner having nights out without you;
- Gifts from another person (items that you haven't bought and haven't seen previously);
- Weekend "work conferences;"
- New aftershave/cologne/perfume;
- Your partner calls you by another name;
- Condoms in your partner's wallet/purse;
- Your partner is easily distracted;
- Your partner being in a daze a lot of the time (thinking about someone else);
- Your partner is being more/less attentive toward you;
- You are suddenly having sex more often;
- You are suddenly having sex less often.

This list is just a suggestion of how someone who is cheating might behave. Look at each of these suggestions as objectively as you can. Don't become paranoid if the answer to some of these questions is YES. The change in your partner could be merely coincidental to your belief that they might be cheating on you. Be as sure as you can possibly be before challenging your partner on these issues.

There are two common threads with regard to jealousy. The first one involves thoughts, feelings, and behavior. The second is when someone feels that their relationship is being threatened.

Ask yourself:

- Have I calmly discussed this issue with my partner?
- Have I identified my justifications and shared these with my partner?
- When I am in a set of circumstances that cause me to feel jealous, does this show in my behavior, either to my partner, or to a third party?

If you haven't already done so, you should find an appropriate time to sit down and calmly talk through your feelings with your partner and allow them the opportunity to clarify (if they can) your unfounded beliefs. You could share your written thoughts with your partner if you so wish. Let your partner read your concerns and address each one in turn in order to relieve and satisfy you.

Having talked to your partner, you will feel:

- Relieved that the issue is out in the open;
- Satisfied that you had, inappropriately, "jumped to conclusions."
- Secure and happy;
- Closer to your partner because your partner has allowed you to be honest and upfront without chastising or condemning you for your belief;
- Able to start afresh because you have "cleared the decks";
- Able to interact and communicate with each other immediately if you think that you have witnessed your partner behaving in an inappropriate way.

This is the outcome you will want, I am sure.

If, however, this is not the case, then you will feel:

- Dissatisfied with the conversation;
- Justified in your belief;
- Angry that your partner has behaved in this way;

...And you may also want:

- A promise from your partner that this behavior will not be repeated;
- To meet with and talk to the third party involved;
- Reassurances from your partner that he/she still loves you despite the indiscretion;
- A trial separation or divorce

These are just some of the feelings and desires that could occur. Everyone's list of outcomes will be different. Should the second list apply to you, then you have the option of "starting over" in your relationship, setting down a set of joint rules that you both agree upon for your future together.

This option might be better achieved by visiting a Marriage Guidance Counselor/Therapist who will help you identify the triggers that prod your jealous feelings and help you overcome these emotions. The worst case scenario would be seeing a Solicitor/Lawyer to arrange for a separation or divorce.

Romantic Jealousy

This usually occurs during the early courtship stage in a relationship.

This feeling can arise when:

- You see your new partner "eyeing up" someone else;
- You think that your new partner is seeing someone else;
- You witness your new partner giving a third party too much attention;

- You feel easily threatened by someone else;
- You think that you love your new partner more than they love you;
- Your new partner does not return your telephone calls;
- Your new partner avoids visiting public places with you (pubs/bars, restaurants, etc.);
- You are told by a "well meaning friend" that they have seen your new partner somewhere that they haven't shared with you;
- Your new partner receives too many text messages;
- Your new partner receives telephone calls that you are not privy to.

This list is endless and unique to each one of us.

If you think that your partner prefers someone else to you, then this will have a detrimental effect on your self-worth. You will feel undermined, intimidated, lacking in confidence, inferior, and inadequate. Your self-esteem is linked to feelings of insecurity and jealousy. Usually, your jealousy says more about you (who you are, how you think, how you behave) than it does about your partner. If in your past relationships you have had just reason to be jealous, then it is important not to bring the negative baggage into a new relationship. In order to "move on" from a previous negative relationship, try this exercise to give yourself the opportunity to re-discover who you are and what you have to offer a new partner.

Ask yourself...

- Do I feel insecure?
- Have I always felt insecure?
- When do I think this insecurity started?
- What am I afraid of?
- Am I afraid of my new partner having friends or meeting mine?

- Am I satisfied with my appearance?
- Am I a good communicator?
- Am I interesting to talk to?
- Are people bored when I talk?
- Am I humorous?
- Am I serious?
- Do I like myself?
- Do I doubt that I can have a good intimate relationship?
- Do I have unspoken expectations of my new partner?

Once again, the list is endless and unique to each of us. Why not set yourself the task of answering all the above questions? Write down your answers. If nothing else, it will help you focus on the most important person in your life—you.

If you bring your past jealousy into your new relationship, be honest with yourself and work through this old habit. If you need the help of a therapist/counselor, don't feel bad about this. It doesn't make you bad, hopeless, or useless. If you think that a therapist can assist you in achieving a positive outcome, and rid you of your bad thinking habits, then ask your medical practitioner to refer you to someone.

Possessive Jealousy

A jealous partner will be possessive and...

- Will tell you how to dress;
- Will be suspicious of where you are and what you are doing when you are not with them;
- Will offer to pick you up from a night out with the girls/lads;
- Will suggest an alternative option (that involves them) if you tell your new partner that you are meeting your friends;

- Will constantly telephone you when you are apart;
- Might stalk you;
- Demanding in their attitude to get what they want;
- Be lacking in the art and skill of communication;
- Will intimidate you with putdowns;
- Is easily aroused to aggression;
- Will always want their own way and can fool you into getting what they want using charm;
- Unreasonable and will use inappropriate behavior;

If you recognize your partner's behavior in any of the above, then forewarned is forearmed. Do not accept this controlling behavior. Decide to challenge your new partner by telling this person that in order for you to proceed in the relationship, they have to understand that you will not be controlled by anyone, and in return, you will not control anyone else. At the onset of a relationship, some of the above behaviors can appear very attractive and endearing. Before too long, however, if you have a jealous partner, you will become consumed with anger, hostility, and resentment at continually being controlled. It will create an unhealthy environment.

If you are the jealous person in the relationship, then being possessive of your partner indicates that you lack confidence and self-worth, and don't trust anyone when they say they love you, probably because you have never learned to love yourself. You might feel that you cannot hold on to your partner unless you have total control and power over them.

Ask yourself...

- Was I loved before I met my new partner?
- Did my parents love me?
- How did they show their love?
- Have I achieved some success in anything I have tried?

- Do I believe that I am unlovable?

All these questions, and more, need answering before you are able to "move on" from drowning in your jealous thoughts. Your existing beliefs are tarnished by past experiences and you must change your thinking patterns from negative to positive. You can try to do this with your new partner if you so wish. However, it would be more productive if you attempted this process with a Therapist/Counselor. I don't believe you should, necessarily, tell your new partner about all your negative past experiences. You don't want to arm them with vital information that they could use against you at a later time in your relationship. Be cautious and prudent about whom you confide in at this time.

If you are living with a jealous partner, and you can identify some of the list as typical of their behavior, then you need to ask yourself, "What am I getting from the relationship?"

Are you getting…?
- Financial security?
- Emotional security?
- Help with domestic chores?
- Help with the children from the partnership (or from previous relationships)?
- Nice vacations?
- Good standard of living: clothes, furniture, house, car, etc.?
- Companionship, friendship, and other positive relationship components?

Or do you stay because you are…?
- Scared of a future without your partner?
- Resigned that you don't want to start over (either alone or with another partner)?

- In a relationship just because you don't want to be alone or single anymore?

Don't fool yourself into believing that you can change your jealous partner. *You cannot*; only they can change themselves. You can, however, decide to change your responses and reactions to the things your new partner demands of you. During the early courtship, both of you are setting precedents for future interactions, demands, and expectations. Learning early on in a new relationship to have an equal set of standards and beliefs will make for a solid foundation upon which to build your relationship.

If you are the jealous partner in a relationship, you must ask yourself why you need to control the person you love.

Some of these issues might be:

- You are scared you will lose your partner;
- You are frightened you will be found out;
- You want emotional security;
- You have lost previous partners through jealousy on your part;
- You want financial security for your future.

This list is only some of the issues. You should make your own.

Emotional Jealousy

Emotional Jealousy is linked to emotional abuse. Emotional abuse is based on insecurity, power, and control.

What are the forms of emotional abuse?

- Not acknowledging someone's presence;
- Resenting someone;
- Repeatedly devaluing someone's feelings;
- Constantly insulting someone;
- Humiliating someone;

- Labeling a person as inferior, stupid, etc.;
- Frightening someone in order to have your own way;
- Constantly threatening someone that you will leave them if they don't do what you tell them;
- Stalking someone;
- Limiting someone's freedom;
- The deliberate act of depriving someone of something that is necessary to obtain a satisfactory quality of life;
- Isolating someone from family or friends;
- Using someone for your own advantage;
- Deliberately failing to care for someone.

Emotional abuse is usually directed at those people who have the least power (e.g., women and children). There is emotional abuse underlying all forms of abuse, and it all leads to mental scarring. The above list contains some examples of emotional abuse. There are many more I am sure you can add to this list.

Emotional jealousy is, in my opinion, linked to a lack of emotional intelligence. To be "emotionally intelligent" is far more important and relevant to healthy living than to be "intellectually intelligent."

What is Emotional Intelligence?

- To have an understanding of yourself, your intentions, your responses, your goals, and your behavior;
- To have a greater understanding of the feelings of other people.

Daniel Goleman, author of *Emotional Intelligence*, identifies the five parts of Emotional Intelligence as:

- Knowing your emotions;
- Managing your emotions;
- Motivating yourself;

- Recognizing and understanding other people's emotions;
- Managing relationships, i.e., managing the emotions of others.

> "Ordinarily, everything we do is in
> our self-interest. Everything."
> Anthony de Mello

When you develop your Emotional Intelligence in the above areas, you become more productive and successful. The outcome of this process is known to reduce stress, decrease conflict, improve relationships, and improve harmony.

Daniel Goleman's framework addresses Emotional Intelligence issues, such as:
- Personal competence;
- Self-awareness;
- Self-motivation;
- Self-regulation;
- Social competence;
- Social awareness;
- Social skills.

Research has shown that people with a strong emotional intelligence have less emotional baggage to contend with. Conversely, people with a low emotional intelligence tend to have more unresolved personal issues.

What are The 7 Habits of Highly Effective People?

Emotional intelligence works well with Stephen Covey's *7 Habits of Highly Effective People*:
- Habit 1: Be Proactive.

This is the ability to control one's environment, rather than have it control you, as is so often the case. Proactive people have self-determination, choice, and the power to decide their own responses to stimuli, conditions, and circumstances.

- Habit 2: Begin With The End In Mind.

Dr. Covey calls this the habit of personal leadership—leading oneself, that is, toward what you consider your aims. By developing the habit of concentrating on relevant activities, you will build a platform to avoid distractions and become more productive and successful.

- Habit 3: Put First Things First.

Dr. Covey calls this the habit of personal management. This is about organizing and implementing activities in line with the aims established in Habit 2. Covey says that Habit 2 is the first, or mental creation; Habit 3 is the second, or physical creation.

- Habit 4 : Think Win-Win.

Dr. Covey calls this the habit of interpersonal leadership, necessary because achievements are largely dependent on co-operative efforts with others. He says that win-win is based on the assumption that there is plenty for everyone, and that success follows a cooperative approach more naturally than the confrontation of win-lose.

- Habit 5: Seek first to understand and then to be understood.

This is one of the great maxims of the modern age. It is Dr. Covey's habit of communication, and is extremely powerful. Dr. Covey helps to explain this in his simple analogy "diagnose before you prescribe." It is simple, effective, and essential for developing, and maintaining positive relationships in all aspects of life.

- Habit 6: Synergy.

Dr. Covey says this is the habit of creative cooperation—the principle that the whole is greater than the sum of its parts, which implicitly lays down the challenge to see the good and potential in the other person's contribution.

- Habit 7: Sharpen the saw.

This is the habit of self-renewal, says Dr. Covey, and it necessarily surrounds all the other habits, enabling and encouraging them to happen and grow. Dr. Covey interprets the self as having four parts: the spiritual, mental, the physical, and the social/emotional, which all need feeding and developing.

You will see from all these explanations that following these suggestions, habits and frameworks will develop and increase your emotional intelligence. This, in turn, will help you to undo emotional jealousy.

Marital Jealousy

At the center of all relationship problems are strong and overpowering emotions:

- Fear that you will be left alone; that your partner will meet someone else who is better than you are;
- Low self-esteem (unworthy of anyone loving you, unconfident, and verbally disabled—can't stick up for yourself);
- Jealousy (angry, unhappy, rejected, hostile, suspicious, holding grudges);
- Abandonment (rejected, isolated, unworthy);
- Hurt (both physical and emotional pain);
- Believing you are unlovable (repeating patterns from past relationships);
- Feeling trapped (I want to break free, but can't get out);
- Desperation (I must make this work, I am nothing without my partner);
- Feeling unloved (no one wants to love me);
- Feeling that you are too ugly to be lovable (this connects to low-self esteem);

- Feeling that you will never find a decent partner (the belief that there are a lot of dogs out there).

You have to consider your emotions in all relationships. Take the emotions away, and there is no relationship.

Let's take a look at the jealous partner's worst emotional fears:

- When my partner touches me, h/she might be thinking of someone else;
- I cannot continue living with the thought that my partner is deceiving me;
- I hate being in my partner's company;
- I am anxious and having panic attacks because of my fears;
- I don't trust my partner;
- My partner ignores me most of the time and never remembers anything that I have said—never mind how important it is;
- I am depressed.

If you believe that all men/women are users and bastards, then these thoughts have a nasty habit of coming absolutely true. Don't underestimate the power of thought. You are what you believe you are. Understand the power of positive thinking. Understand the power of a positive attitude. Imagine releasing these negative thoughts.

Sit down and create an image whereby you release your worst fears. Stay in that slightly hypnotic state and dream yourself into thinking healthily. Isn't it good to have those burdens lifted and erased? You can be in this state of freedom all of the time if you choose to tackle your negative thinking habits. In my opinion, you can more easily do this with the help of a therapist/counselor, although many people, including me, have managed to achieve this "normal and balanced" state alone.

Responsibility (if you are the jealous partner)

- Accept and take responsibility for being jealous;
- Accept that in order to move on and live in a loving healthy relationship, you must let go of the jealousy you feel;
- Make a commitment to deal with this issue;
- Let go of the hurt and pain that is destroying you and your relationship;
- Stop acting miserable, regardless of what you feel inside. The choice of how you act is yours alone to make;
- Accept the love you want;
- Acknowledge your fears but refuse to be paralyzed by them. Courage is nothing more than being afraid but acting anyways;
- Let go of compulsive worrying. Let's face it; none of us can predict what will happen tomorrow. No amount of worrying can change the future;
- Learn to trust your partner.

In order to move on from jealousy, you need to learn to recognize your jealous thoughts immediately when you think them, and stop them in their tracks. Daniel D. Amen, M.D., popularized the notion of managing these Automatic Negative Thoughts (or ANTs) in his groundbreaking book *Change Your Brain, Change Your Life*.

We all talk to ourselves all the time (mind chatter). If your mind chatter is full of negative, jealous fantasies/stories (such as your partner running off with your neighbor, or that your partner is having an affair), you will keep on regurgitating the same old negative stories time after time after time. Also, if you are jealous when someone pays particular interest to your partner, talking and laughing with them, your creative mind will devise negative jealous stories and images around the possibility and likelihood of these stories actually happening.

Your mind cannot determine whether or not these stories are true, so it will continually come up with these negative jealous scenarios that you will start to believe. These negative, jealous stories will magnify in your mind and overtake the reality of the situation. It is because this happens that you have, and will, give your partner a bad time over quite innocently chatting and laughing with someone. You must learn to separate what's really happening, in the here and now, and not allow your creative mind to link in to fears that are based on your past experiences. When you can do this, and also stopping your jealous thoughts, you will be on your way to emotional freedom.

Ways to Overcome Your Jealousy

- Being clear in your communications with your partner;
- Stopping your trait of being afraid of outcomes;
- Being courageous;
- Being honest;
- Deciding to clear out issues that you have been hanging on to;
- Believing in yourself;
- Learning to love yourself;
- Challenging your thoughts (prior to speaking, ask yourself, is that the right way to think and respond);
- Stopping the habit of living in the past;
- Learning to live in the "now;"
- Clearing out your old belief patterns.

Life will be difficult if you are living with a jealous partner. Understand that if your partner recognizes that their jealous feelings are destructive and unfounded, then you are on your way to eliminating jealousy from your relationship. The first step for them is accepting that they are jealous.

Discuss (honest communication is the key here) everything with your partner and encourage and support any changes they make. You will need to acquire some patience during this time, as this will be a slow process. Don't forget that your partner has been jealous for a long time and, therefore, it will not go overnight. No one is born jealous. It is learned from experiencing emotional pain. Learn to identify the triggers that bring the jealous thoughts into reality. Learn to trust each other.

If your partner will not accept that s/he is jealous, you are battling with the situation alone. There is no way a relationship can survive if the jealous partner cannot see and admit that they are causing the relationship to fail with their consistent persecution directed at you. Perhaps your partner would agree to see a Marriage Guidance Counselor. If you can get your partner to agree to this, then there is a chance that the relationship will survive and develop normally. Counselors are skilled at unearthing the truth and do this in a subtle way.

Another idea might be to ask a friend or family member your partner trusts and co-opt their help in assisting you in your quest. If all this fails, then you are left with more of the same behavior that you are experiencing. Research has shown that when the jealous person's emotional pain gets bad enough, they will surrender and give the jealousy up because living with the jealous thoughts will eventually reduce them to emotional wrecks. However, in the meantime, there is something you can do to alleviate the pain of jealousy you are feeling, and that is to begin changing your reactions and responses to your partner's accusations.

Guidelines for Changing Your Reactions:

- Stay calm;
- Decide not to react;

- Decide to think before you speak;
- Decide to give your partner the opportunity to tell the story they are having difficulty with, and then tell them the story as you see it;
- Refuse to argue;
- If you discover you have entered an argument, refuse to keep the momentum of it going;
- Try and change your reaction and response by using words or phrases that you haven't used before during this type of discussion. For example, your partner says, "I saw you flirting, talking, and laughing with Chris," your response is, "Yes, I was talking to Chris and the next time I am in a similar situation, either with Chris or anyone else, I will look around for you so that you too can join in."
- Show your partner how much you love him/her;
- Be as supportive as you can be;
- Remember other incidents that have been similar, which proved to be unfounded, repeat these to your partner in an effort for him/her to see that they have no cause to be jealous;
- If the story and situation of the jealousy includes a third party, suggest to your partner that you invite this person to your home to calmly discuss the issue. This will at least show your partner that you have no problem or embarrassment confronting this problem with the person your partner has identified as the cause.

There is no easy route if your partner continues being jealous. A young lady I knew agreed to take part in a lie detector test to prove to her partner that she had not been cheating on him. The test result was in her favor. This marriage was fine for a few weeks after the test, but then jealousy returned. Her husband became convinced that his wife knew how to fool the lie detector machine. This situation continued for some time after this episode with his wife subjugating herself to her husband's violent behavior. Finally the marriage ended.

> "Learning to be aware of feelings, how they arise and how to use them creatively so they guide us to happiness, is an essential lifetime skill."
>
> Joan Borysenko

Financial Jealousy

Beliefs you may have:
- Other people have more money than you;
- Other people have two homes (a holiday home); why can't you?
- Other people earn more than you do;
- Other people can make themselves look more attractive as they are able to purchase designer clothes, etc.;
- Other people have nicer cars than you have;
- Other people can eat out at expensive, smart restaurants where you can't afford to eat;
- Other people have better jobs;
- Other people "get all the luck;"
- Other people have private healthcare and why can't you?
- Other people have had a private education and are therefore better than you.

Surveys carried out have identified that for men, the most distressful situation was a partner having an affair with someone of higher financial status. For women, the focus of distress was a partner having an affair with someone who is more attractive.

There will always be someone who has more of everything that you have. Accept that fact and put it to one side. Concentrate on how you can improve your financial status, if that is what you want. I believe I speak for most women when I say that what they yearn for most in the relationship with their partner is love and faithfulness. Western traditions confirm that men are "the breadwinners" of the relationship and therefore they may feel more pressure to provide for the family than women do. I am keen to put this notion in perspective. Don't forget money can't buy you love and it can't buy you good health.

Material Jealousy

Material Jealousy runs parallel with Financial Jealousy. Material jealousy is when you covet another's belongings. Concentrate instead on yourself and what you have. Count your blessings and stop focusing on what you can't have. Judging people by what they own is superficial. Concentrate on what you have got and what you can get by using your own creativity and skills.

Jealousy of Children

A parent can be jealous of a child or children. This is so whether the child is their biological child or a stepchild. How many times have I heard someone say "My partner always puts the children first?" And my comment is, "rightly so." It is important for adults to understand that the love a parent has for a child is very different from the love between committed adults. In this scenario, no one comes first. How can one be first when both loves are so dramatically different?

Of course, a child's needs come before a partner's needs. If the child is hungry, he/she should be fed. If a child is tired, he/she should be bathed and put to bed. If a child is ill, the attention of the parent naturally falls to looking after the child. What's the problem? A person who has low self-esteem may try to deny the child to be first place in a parent's affection. Although this behavior may appear selfish to the outside observer, it is really the case that the partner is unconsciously trying to make up for a lack they themselves felt in childhood. Unfortunately, the strategy both doesn't work and is harmful to all the current family dynamics. It is during childhood that infants and toddlers learn who they are. They learn this through their interactions with parents, siblings, extended family, friends, etc.

Unconscious questions children may have:
- Am I important in this home?
- Can I depend on my mommy or daddy?
- If I cry, will I get smacked?
- Do these people like me?
- Am I doing OK?
- Should I be scared of mommy or daddy?
- Can I have a tantrum and get away with it?
- Should I behave like this?
- What am I doing that's wrong?
- What am I doing that's right?

The everyday communication you have with your children shape who they are and how people respond to them. They are like sponges absorbing every nuance, action, and reaction that goes on around them. When a child has good, constant nurturing and is shown love and affection, you are providing them with a yardstick to show them how to measure love in the future. You are showing them what they can, and should, expect from others as they go through life. If they are denied this love as a child, they will have learned from their parents that love is in short supply now and in the future. It places a huge responsibility on parents to be loving, constant, fair, disciplined, and competent in handling a child's early developmental stages.

Parents are the guides that children look to, to find out what type of behavior is acceptable and what type of behavior is unacceptable. This is the most important reason that the top priority for a couple experiencing jealousy issues should be to not quarrel, argue, disagree, fight (physically or emotionally) in the child's presence or earshot. I know this can be difficult to achieve, but this rule should be adhered to at all times if the parents want their children to become enthusiastic, energetic, loving, friendly, ambitious, and positive adults. Regardless of how a parent feels inside, the action in front of the children should be such that the child learns to be realistically trusting, being able to give and receive love, etc. That is, act in a way you want your child to be when grown. In fact, a program of doing this will eventually change the pathological thinking patterns, because habits are changed by behavior.

If one parent is jealous of the child, then their resulting behavior and attitude with the child will be strained, non-communicative, destructive, and carrying many other negative emotional responses. Recognize that your behavior will be the stuff your child forms future relationships upon. Look back to your own childhood. Were you raised in a loving home? If you were, then you will understand and agree with this statement. If you were not, then you might be able to understand the detrimental effect your childhood has had in you forming loving relationships as an adult.

What can you do, as a parent, to ensure that you child is raised in a loving home?

- Give your child your time;
- Give your child attention;
- Be constant and dependable;
- Keep your promises;

- Interact with them by reading stories, drawing pictures, and allowing them to help with domestic chores or DIY things;
- Give them some responsibility for themselves or pets (small stuff at first);
- Never shout and scream at them;
- Teach them that calm discussion can result in a positive outcome;
- Cuddle them;
- Respect them because they are people with needs just like you. For example, if they are hungry and the next family meal is some time away, make them a snack to show them you care about them;
- Provide your child with opportunities to decide some things for themselves with your guidance. Ask them, "What would you like to eat?" You are providing the foundation for the basic decision-making skills;
- Have realistic expectations;
- Teach them to share their toys with other children;
- When using the bathroom, take the child with you until they are old enough to understand that you are going out of the room but will be back soon;
- Focus on your child;
- Remember that if your own needs are being met, you will be better placed to carry out the needs of your child. Look after yourself and try to stick to "household rules" that both of you (parents) have decided upon.

Parents are people too, and they don't have to be perfect. This list is an ideal. Do your best to live up to it. When you slip (as everyone does sometimes), apologize, correct the situation, forgive yourself, and move on.

Work-Related Jealousy

Professional jealousy is rife, with one person trying to out-do their fellow worker with no regard for the personal consequences of their actions, such as, stress, depression, and anxiety. Surveys have shown that almost 9 out of 10 office workers suffer from professional jealousy, believing that their colleagues have more glamorous and better paid jobs.

What do you need to do to overcome professional jealousy?

- Increase your self-confidence, self-esteem, and self-worth.

- Reinforce your feelings of personal well-being;

- You need to reinforce your belief in your capabilities;

- Explore past working experiences in order to identify your trigger points that lead to professional jealousy;

- Trust your own judgment on professional issues; avoid endless loops of second-guessing;

Consider that being professionally jealous may have led you to avoid challenges because you fear failing and looking foolish. Thus, you therefore stay where you are, and fuel jealous of your colleagues who are not afraid to "have a go."

Many people feel professional jealousy. You can, however, ensure that your response to that feeling is controlled and constructive. Accept the feeling, control the feeling, and move on from the feeling.

Sibling Jealousy

Sibling rivalry is a real condition that can erode childhood relationships and continue to destroy the relationship into adulthood, if it is handled without sensitivity and care. The jealousy occurs when the second child is born.

This is an example of sibling jealousy:

When a new child is born, you reduce the attention you give the older child because babies need constant attention. The older child might see this display of constant attention to the baby as mommy preferring the younger child. Your older child loves you the same amount as before the baby was born, but now has to share your time and attention. It's a foreign feeling to the older child, who doesn't understand why this is happening. If the older child is of an age that he/she can communicate their feelings, they might say something like, "Why did you have the baby; is it because I have done something wrong or that you don't love me anymore?" Eventually, the older child will learn to love the baby, but initially the new baby is tolerated and seen as an intruder.

Second and third children can feel sibling jealousy also. As they grow, they notice that the older child can do things they can't; is allowed to go to bed later; has toys and possessions they are not allowed to have, and so on. The onus is on how the parents handle the situation rather than whether it happens to a first, second, or third child.

What can you do to fix this situation?

- You can remember to include and involve all your children in the birth of a new baby;

- You can give each child a small task involving the new arrival (putting talcum powder on the baby's bottom is an example);

- You can observe and acknowledge any negative reaction by your children to the arrival of the baby; if you can see it, react by reinforcing (with words and deeds) that you love them all equally;

- You can pay special attention to the older children. Remember that a newborn baby can comfortably sleep

for a long period of time. This gives you the opportunity of focusing your attention on the older children.

Typically, the mother is with the children for much of the
day, with father at work. So, father's time is more highly valued by the children. This can be used for the children's
benefit. One way is to have the father institute a regular system of one-on-one child time. When they are infants, this can
be father bathing the baby, then putting the older one to bed.
Later, it can be father reading each child a book. Later still, it
can be a half-day, and then a full day, devoted by father to
being with that one child, doing an activity a child has
planned. Such special times can be once a month or even less
frequently. The lead time allows the child to anticipate it,
think about it, and plan it.

Violent Jealousy

Violent jealousy is quite simply physical abuse. These behaviors might begin with throwing or smashing objects
during an argument (assault). Or it might start with pushing
and shoving and lead to hitting or choking (battery). In severe
cases, it may end with murder, intentional or not. All these
types of behaviors can make the affected partner feel powerless, confused, isolated, trapped, worthless, angry, or even
crazy.

You are living with violent jealousy if your partner is...

- Physically violent with you;
- Constantly angry at you or him/herself;
- Frustrated with him/herself;
- Blaming you for everything that goes wrong;
- Possessive of you;
- Intimidating or dominating you;
- Often interrogating you;
- Critical of you;

And much more. Remember you don't have to put up with this behavior. You always have the option of separating/divorcing. However, John Gottman's research shows there are two types of physical abusers. Type 1 abusers are likely to respond to attempts at separation with murder, so it's not necessarily that simple. The woman needs to plan the separation very carefully. If you have had violence done to you or received the threat of violence, you are advised to contact your nearest Domestic Violence Support center for advice before acting (see Appendix).

Pathological/Morbid Jealousy and Insane Jealousy

This is sometimes called "delusional jealousy." The important part to this type of jealousy is the delusion that the pathological/ morbidly jealous partner feels that their partner is being unfaithful. This belief has no evidence to substantiate the accusation and no logical argument. The pathological/ morbidly jealous person searches relentlessly for conflict, and their belief is based on flimsy evidence. The essential difference between pathological/morbid jealousy and so-called "normal" jealousy is that a normal person will express jealousy only where there is clear evidence and when the situation is thrust upon them, while the pathological/morbid person regards even slight signs as conclusive evidence of unfaithfulness, and reacts forcefully.

The pathological/morbidly jealous person will try to find out, by any means they can, that their partner is having an affair, and even though no evidence emerges, the pathological/morbidly jealous partner will not be satisfied. The partner who is the "victim" can usually identify with their partner's type of jealousy and can feel sorry for them. This reaction, by women in particular, who are battered by their partners, might explain why they try to protect them and even try to justify their behavior. A person diagnosed as being pathologically/morbidly jealous can be dangerous by lashing out against their innocent partner. This condition can be secondary to a schizophrenic state.

This type of jealousy can manifest itself by the jealous partner persistently torturing their innocent partner by continually interrogating them as to:

- Where are you going?
- Where have you been?
- Who have you spoken to?
- Who are you having an affair with?

The above is a small sample of the questions. I am sure you will add to this list. This relentless interrogation and intimidation will emotionally disable both the jealous partner and the innocent partner. The quality of life for both partners will be negligible. Thousands of women (particularly) are living in this situation where they are afraid of their partners and feel they cannot confide in or seek help in fear of their partner finding out. Many morbid/pathological/insane jealous people and/or their partners will turn to drink and drugs as a means of coping in these circumstances. Jealousy can underlie depression, anxiety, panic, low self-esteem, and low confidence. If some or all of the above is your current situation, then both you and your jealous partner need to seek professional help to unearth and identify the underlying emotions linked to this type of jealousy so as to get the opportunity to move on in life without this destructive emotion recurring in your relationship.

> "Jealousy is all the fun you think they had."
> Erica Jong

4 Possessive/Jealous Men in Relationships

A possessive/jealous man will:

- Tell you how to dress;
- Be overly concerned about where you are going when socializing;
- Insist on escorting you to mundane places;
- Interfere or veto your social plans;
- Make excessive phone calls to know your whereabouts;
- Be intense about everything;
- Be unable to communicate and discuss anything with you;
- Put you down and will do anything to make you feel inferior;
- Have a negative outlook and poor self-esteem/lack of confidence;
- Be dominant in domestic arrangements;
- Be aggressive and display an unreasonable attitude to minor details.

The above list is some of the characteristics to look for in respect of identifying a possessive/jealous man in advance. Often, he may be good-looking with plenty of charisma and charm and oozing apparent self-confidence. At this stage of the "love game," you will have no reason to suspect that he is any other than the way he portrays himself. Generally, once a possessive/jealous man finds his woman, he does not believe he can keep her. He believes that his woman will be taken from him by another man. This is largely due to a lack of confidence, poor self-esteem, and limited or no self-respect. The possessive/jealous man does not believe that he deserves to have a partner who loves them. He will not be able to trust his partner and will not believe her words of love.

He will be more likely to believe that his woman is only with him until she finds a better partner. Because of this lack of self-belief, this man will unconsciously set about creating scenarios where he can control his partner, making his partner stay with him and depend on him. This is where their value on themselves lies, in the misguided belief that their partner cannot do without them. When your possessive partner has achieved what he has set out to create—a dependent woman—he will start the process of undermining you.

He will:

- Criticize everything you say and do;
- Make you feel bad about yourself;
- Undermine your confidence;
- Tell you constantly how lucky you are to have him;
- Make you believe that no-one else would have you.

If you felt good about yourself at the onset of the relationship, a few months down the road you will begin to feel insecure and will suffer from low self-esteem. This is precisely where your partner wants you to be. He has built up a dependency and a fear in you that makes you believe that you are nothing and nobody without him. You will forget who you really are, a confident, capable person, and you will become a "Stepford wife," that is someone who caters completely, with no questions asked, to your partner's needs and desires.

He will need constant demonstration and proof that you love him. No matter what you say and do, he will distrust you and will believe you have a hidden agenda or other motives for telling him that you love him. Family and friends will see the difference in you, and may tell you that you have changed. When you innocently repeat this to your husband/partner, he will think that there is a conspiracy between you all to take you away from him. The remarks made by your family and friends will be ignored as you continue along the path of totally believing what your possessive partner is telling you. After all, "why would they lie to you and do this to you?" Soon, you will be in a position where you are isolated from those people who love and care for you.

A dominant parental environment can produce men who lack self-respect, who are unable to adequately contribute to domestic chores and who are frustrated with their careers and also have no financial security. They do not believe they are "masculine men."

A confident man with no possessive hang-ups does not have a problem with possessive jealousy. This man is someone who celebrates his partner's independence, beliefs, and values. He will know that relationships are about trust, caring, and sharing. He happily accepts his partner's views without recriminations. He knows that love will not grow by smothering and choking your partner. It will grow by trusting, honest, open communication.

Women are becoming powerful in the work arena and are more confident in other aspects of their lives. This fact will disempower some men who believe that a woman's place is in the home, or most certainly beneath him.

The Jealous/Possessive Man

This man goes through torment and torture every day of his life. He is insecure and has no personal control. He usually has no friends and is even quite isolated in his work (you can be alone even in a crowd). If this jealous man is in a relationship with you, then at the onset of the relationship, you will feel totally loved and treasured by him. Nothing will be too much trouble. He will do anything and everything for you.

Another variation is the "alpha male," with a belief of entitlement and ownership, who feels a compulsion to dominate in any situation. To them, their woman is a possession to be guarded. They are often very popular and charming, and friends flock to them.]

However, once he has gained your trust and commitment, he will gradually change and:

- He will become suspicious and distrustful;
- He will try to find a hidden meaning in every word you say;
- He will limit your visits to friends and family and, most likely, he will want to come with you. His ultimate aim will be to isolate you from everyone in your past;
- He will be upset if you arrange to do anything without him being present;
- He will be overly attentive and you will feel smothered;
- He will expect you to totally believe him and do everything he asks of you;
- He will take control of all financial issues;
- He will expect you (and your children) to abide by his word;
- He will expect you to ask his permission before doing anything;
- He will be mean with the amount of money he allocates to you;
- He will embarrass you in public;
- He will always be on the lookout to see if you are interested in other men.

If you are the jealous man reading this, you might be able to add more statements that are unique to you. If you are living with a jealous man, you will see some of your man's traits in this list.

Where does your jealousy come from?

- Your childhood;
- Past relationships;
- Fear;
- Insecurity;
- Being too pampered as a child;
- Being ignored as a child;
- A lack of self-respect;
- Being too controlled as a child;
- Anxiety;
- Depression;
- Being overlooked for promotion in the workplace;
- Believing that your partner will leave you;
- Believing that you aren't getting enough attention from your partner.

Indeed, jealousy can arise from many events during the course of your life. You all have choices open to you. You have a choice to stay jealous. You have a choice to overcome jealousy. I hope you will choose the latter.

Ways to help overcome your jealousy:

- Be patient;
- Be prepared for some hard work;
- Learn to be realistic;
- Identify the triggers that set you off in your jealous thoughts;
- Revisit your childhood – look at your role models and the environment you were raised in;
- Remind yourself that your partner loves you;
- Learn to love and accept yourself;
- Look at your behavior and attitude;

- Learn to trust;
- Use positive self-talk (we all talk to ourselves in our mind — mind chatter — this talking to yourself should be *positive*);
- Rid yourself of bad, old repeating patterns of behavior (these are the negative thoughts that keep on and on in your mind, guiding you to believe that you are right to be jealous);
- Enlist the cooperation of your partner;
- Ask your partner for gentle reassurances;

The above list will help you to overcome your jealous habit.

I have suggested that the jealous partner should change the negative thoughts that are constantly in their mind. I have written in depth about this process in my book, *Life After Your Lover Walks Out: A Practical Guide*. However, I will give you a brief description of how you can achieve a change of thought process.

Your mind records mental pictures of everything you have experienced. If these thoughts are mostly negative, then you will repeat the negative reactions you have always used. Irrational reaction comes from irrational thought. The sequence is: first comes the thought, the next step is the feeling, and then the final step is the action. Your irrational, reactive mind makes you say and do things that are not really you. They are just automatic responses that you have always used and never thought to challenge. This is why you sometimes react in ways you do not understand but later regret.

Learn from these errors and stop reacting and being spontaneous. Instead, think before you speak. Change your reactions. Know that your responses up to now have not benefited you in any way. In fact, you will probably agree that they have caused mayhem within you and within your relationship.

Your mind is your best asset and your worst liability. It can be a powerful source of creativity or a powerful force of destruction.

Decide that:

- You are in charge of your mind;
- You are in charge of your thoughts, actions, and reactions;
- You are personally responsible and accountable for all that you think, say, and do.

The range of emotions jealousy exhibits are:

- Pain
- Anger
- Rage
- Sadness
- Resentment

- Worry
- Grief
- Fear
- Humiliation
- Envy

The above emotions result in the following behavior:

- Aggressive actions and reactions
- Violence
- Constant unreasonable questioning
- Panic attacks
- Controlling

…And many more unwanted behaviors.

It is important to remember that unless you have a very good reason to be jealous, you should not keep on at your partner with these thoughts.

Remember that your partner chose *you!* Don't make your partner sorry that they did choose you by behaving in an unreasonable, inappropriate way. Jealousy destroys the thing it tries to protect. The object of your love will stop loving you if treated in the way jealousy leads you. So, however you feel inside, treat the other person in a way designed to foster love, not to destroy it.

Things you should avoid doing:

- Controlling your partner;
- Being aggressive;
- Obsessing about jealous thoughts in your head—if you remind yourself to think positive thoughts when this happens, you will eventually develop a habit of doing this;
- Pushing your partner away from you with your behavior
- Keeping all these thoughts to yourself—share these thoughts with your partner in the context of asking for their help in overcoming these thoughts

Things you can start doing now:

- Becoming a trusted friend to your partner;
- Trusting your partner;
- Allowing your partner to have his/her own friends and hobbies;
- Allowing your partner to visit family without you always being present;

If you are able to do some of the things on this suggested list, you will soon see that you can choose not to be jealous and your life will be happier as a result of these exercises.

A small amount of jealousy in a relationship can be positive and reassuring, but it is essential to keep jealousy under strict control.

> "You can't teach anybody anything, only make them realize the answers are already inside them."
>
> Galileo

5	**Possessive/Jealous Women in Relationships**

How can you identify a possessive woman? Here are some indicators.

A possessive woman will...

- Become unpleasant or get nasty if you spend too much time with family, friends, or indeed anyone other than her;
- Want to know where you are all of the time;
- Constantly ring you on your cell phone;
- Make sure that you have jobs to do around the house in order to keep you in her sight;
- Resort to emotional blackmail (saying she has a headache/backache/feels sick) in order to keep you at home with her;
- Make all social arrangements for both of you with people that she feels comfortable with;
- Be very uncomfortable if an attractive woman talks to you, works with you, sits next to you, etc.;
- Search through your cell phone for unknown numbers, search through your wallet for credit cards, and search through your clothing for receipts or telltales;
- Rummage around in your office when you are not there. She might not know what she is looking for, but she will do it anyway "just in case";
- Become verbally and physically abusive;

If you are the jealous woman, the things to avoid doing are the same list as in Step 4 (Possessive men). Please re-read this list and apply it to yourself.

What can the partner of a jealous woman do about it?

- Reassure her;
- Try and help her find the root cause of her jealousy;
- Communicate with her and tell her exactly what you are about, so that you can show her you have nothing to hide;
- Show her love and affection and make her feel special;
- Sign up with her to a therapist to help you sort out this issue;
- Help her unravel her fears;
- Encourage her to believe in you.

Are you the jealous woman? Your continuing unreasonable jealousy and distrust can result in a breakdown in the relationship. Refer to Step 3 and use the information on repeating patterns of behavior. Try it out. It does work. Be diligent, you owe it to yourself and your partner.

Facial expressions and what they say about you

I believe that women are more likely to show their feelings on their face than to speak them. A woman doesn't have to say what she thinks, as the recipient can read her face quite easily. Of course, some men are bad at hiding their feelings also.

Some examples of facial expressions:

- Surprise
- Fear
- Sadness
- Contempt
- Disgust
- Anger
- Enjoyment

In any interaction between people, but particularly in an intimate relationship, I believe it is useful to both listen to what your partner is saying and also to read the message that your partner is projecting to you from their facial expressions. Often you will see that, whilst your partner is verbally agreeing with you, their face is telling you that they blatantly disagree with what you are saying or doing. Acknowledging facial expressions and body language can make all the difference between understanding and misunderstanding. Of course, clarifying questions are even better because one can misread nonverbal signals as much as words.

By learning to identify the facial expressions of your partner, you will both learn to identify the real feeling underneath the spoken words. If you can identify your partner's emotions early on, you will be better equipped to deal with situations that arise in your relationship. This will result in better communication that will assist you in overcoming jealousy.

Learn to recognize two types of subtle signs:

Light, subtle glimpses: These expressions are very brief and last for a split second. Everyone who shows a less subtle expression is trying, consciously or subconsciously, to hide their true feelings. For example, perhaps your partner is trying to hide the anger they feel about an issue you are discussing. If you are lucky and you spot the subtle expression on your partner's face, you get a brief glimpse of what your partner is really feeling.

Heavier glimpses: These expressions are usually a second or so longer, but they are often missed because they are so difficult to identify. Subtle expressions occur when an emotion is just beginning to build and also when your partner is trying to conceal it in order, perhaps, to not upset you.

Learn to observe and identify your partner's facial expressive communication to you. This ability is an invaluable tool that will assist you in your personal and professional relationships.

Here are some examples of how anger is shown on the face:

- Anger changes the color in the face. It can take on a lighter (white) or darker color (red);

- Anger can dry the mouth, which in turn makes the top lip stuck to the upper teeth (baring their teeth);

- Anger is seen in the eyes. They can become wide and wild or small and piercing;

- Anger is seen by the overall appearance of someone ready to pounce;

All these facial signs will be helpful to both partners in order to be immediately aware that something is amiss and therefore avoid unnecessary disagreements and arguments.

> "Consult not your fears but your hopes and your dreams. Think not about your frustrations, but about your unfulfilled potential. Concern yourself not with what you tried and failed in, but with what it is still possible for you to do."
>
> — Pope John XXIII

6 | Restructuring Your Relationship After the Pain of Jealousy

Restructuring

What does restructuring mean in this context? It simply means that in order to move on from being jealous, you must change the way you think, change your behavior, and also change your attitude.

The feeling of jealousy in a relationship reveals that part of us which we would prefer to remain hidden.

What are these feelings and how are they displayed?

- Anger at not being understood, which leads on to shouting/blaming/swearing/violence;
- Hostility because you don't want to be made a fool of, which leads to bitterness and withdrawing from your partner;
- Feelings of humiliation at the way you have behaved, which can lead on to revenge/getting your own back;
- Shame that you cannot accept and trust, which leads on to not liking yourself, feeling ugly, and lowering the value you place on yourself.

These are only some of the things that are happening during the jealous period you are experiencing.

What are the things you should be saying and doing?

If you believe you are misunderstood by your partner, you should replace anger with patience, using a soft, calm voice to explain exactly how you feel. Threats and shouting get you nowhere. Don't overdramatize the situation.

If you feel you are being made a fool of, share this with your partner in a sensible, calm way. Don't withdraw from your partner. You will not get anywhere that way but will make the gap between you wider.

If you feel humiliated by your own actions, tell your partner how you feel. With honest communication between you, your partner might accept what you are saying and change his/her behavior.

If you feel ashamed of your behavior and you share this with your partner, then you will be giving your partner the opportunity to understand you on a deeper level. If, however, you feel ashamed of your partner's behavior, then you must tell him/her about this. If you don't share your feelings, particularly at this stage of restructuring your relationship, you both will be unable to put your relationship on a better footing.

In any verbal interaction with your partner, avoid words like *always* and *never*. These words imply that your partner is always doing or saying something (which is rarely the case) and if you say "You never remember anything I say," it implies that your partner does not consider you at all (again this is rarely the case). It is very important to understand that words uttered cannot be changed. Words are powerful and, as such, should be thought out and used carefully. You will not be able to retract the words you use without some considerable effort and explanation.

Example: The New Bed

This is the case of a lady who bought a new bed. On the day the bed was delivered, her husband took a day off work to dismantle the old bed and assemble the new bed. The bed was delivered at 2 p.m. On arriving home at 5 p.m., this lady went straight upstairs, excited to see her new bed fully assembled, only to discover her husband sitting cross-legged inside the frame of the bed, hammering screws into the frame (the screws should have been screwed in but her husband didn't have the patience or interest to do this).

In the past, this lady would have flown into a rage and accused her husband of being useless; "you are pathetic and stupid" is the phrase she had used. Instead, mindful of the consequences of the old phrases, she said, "you're doing a good job, and I recognize that I couldn't do it. She left the room and went to her office in the attic to (a) get out of his way and (b) she found the scene funny and didn't want to upset her husband by laughing as he would have interpreted her laughter as poking fun at him rather than seeing the situation with humor.

While she was upstairs in the office, she could hear her husband ranting and raving and calling himself useless. In previous situations such as this, she would have stayed in the room with her husband while he tackled the job in hand, and she would have been frightened and upset by his antics (he had never been physically violent with her, but he had intimated, controlled, and threatened her in the past).

To add insult to injury, this lady had made arrangements with her friends to have a meal with them that evening, so off she toddled to meet her friends. On arriving at the restaurant, she received a phone call from her husband who yelled, "Get home now, I have broken the bed" (he used more colorful language than that). She calmly replied, "No." This situation in the past would have had her return home immediately, because she would have been scared of the consequences otherwise. On this occasion, she stayed in the restaurant with her friends and enjoyed her time with them.

When she eventually returned home, her husband was in a dour mood, watching the television. He gave her short answers to her light-hearted questions, so she ran upstairs to find the bed fully assembled, complete with bedclothes. She returned to the living room and congratulated her husband on doing a good job.

The same scenario but seeing it from the point of view of the husband:

He thought, "The new bed is being delivered today. I hope the delivery men will assemble it for me because I'm useless on do-it-yourself projects and will only make a mess of it." When the bed was delivered, the men shot off and left this guy to assemble the bed on his own. There were massive cardboard boxes everywhere and he didn't know how or where to start. When in situations such as this, he always panicked and perspired profusely.

He was angry that there was no one he could turn to for help. Why wasn't there anyone to turn to? Because he had alienated his close family by his possessive, unreasonable behavior. They had only tolerated him until they were old enough to move out and lead their own lives. He was stuck with this gigantic task of putting the bed together alone. He unpacked all the boxes and started structuring the frame, screwing screws into the frame, etc. All the time he was doing this task, he was swearing and stamping around and fully aware that his ability to do a good job was very limited.

When his wife returned home from work, she ran upstairs to see her new bed. He was angry and disappointed with himself that he hadn't completed the task, so that she could see how well he had done and admire his handiwork. Instead, she was greeted by him swearing and blaming her for buying a new bed when she knew he was useless at "DIY" stuff. He was aware that his wife made herself scarce and scurried off to her office in the attic to avoid witnessing this ridiculous, angry scene.

Later on, she went out and he felt abandoned by her and completely unsupported by her leaving him alone and going out. He telephoned her several times and on one occasion yelled, "Get home now!" When she said, "No," he was shocked. He couldn't understand why she wasn't obeying his commands as she always used to. He ploughed on grudgingly and completed the assembling of the bed. His wife returned later and he was determined to make her suffer for leaving him alone in this task. He became aware that his wife wasn't responding to his mood by pussyfooting around him as she usually did, and he decided he should react differently to her and began answering her questions with slightly more enthusiasm.

The point of this story is that if you don't dare to change your reactions when your partner is in a mood/jealous/hostile, etc., you are colluding with them to stay the same. Both of you take some baby steps and try and change your interaction with each other. You have nothing to lose and everything to gain from attempting this task.

Problem Solving

In order to be adept at problem solving, you must learn to have honest, clear communication skills. Without communication skills, you will be unable to discuss issues positively or work out solutions to problems that will arise.

What essential tools are needed for productive problem solving?

- A clear head
- A non-judgmental attitude
- The ability to allow you both to express your feelings
- Patience, tolerance, and understanding
- A clear description of the problem
- Taking ownership of the problem
- A clear understanding of what will be the outcome if the problem is not solved
- Have a clear understanding of how the problem impacts on both partners and others
- Be able to identify whether you or your partner, or both of you have the problem

- Identify both positive and negative aspects of the problem
- Identify how important the problem is and be able to prioritize the task of dealing with it
- Both get involved and find different ways of handling the problem (brainstorming)
- Identify alternative approaches to the problem and follow through each alternative approach to its conclusion in order to see the consequences of each alternative

Each of you must deal with the problem alone, finding ways to handle the issue, and then share your answers with your partner. By doing this, each partner will feel valued and will gain self-respect in attempting to solve the problem alone. When you come together, discuss both answers to their ultimate conclusion and perhaps a compromise will be appropriate.

> "Do not feed your ego and your problems, with your attention. ...Slowly, surely, the ego will lose weight, until one fine day it will be nothing but a thin ghost of its former self. You will be able to see right through it, to the divine presence that shines in each of us."
>
> -- Eknath Easwaran

Barriers to Problem Solving

Below are some examples of barriers that are unproductive in problem solving:

- A fear of saying something wrong
- Resentment of having to solve the problem, believing that it isn't your fault anyway
- Being inflexible and unable to adapt to problem solving techniques
- Staying in the role of "victim"

- Being too dominant
- Denial that there is a problem
- One or both partners always believing they are right
- Being too stressed, anxious, or depressed to take part in problem solving
- Being closed-minded to new ideas
- Being stuck in the rut of the problem
- Not being able to "think outside the box," that is to say that all alternatives should be looked at, however bizarre they at first appear to be
- Feeling of wasting your time, as it is clearly not your problem
- Being too tired, too lethargic, or too disinterested in the problem
- Being too angry or hostile to deal with the problem
- Agreeing to do certain things to address the problem only if the outcome is to your advantage
- Not sticking to the problem (bringing other issues into the discussion)
- One or both partners interrupting when points are aired
- Discussing past issues and throwing up incidents of your partner's bad behavior
- Trying to second guess what your partner is going to say

Here are some examples of things to discuss when problem solving:

- The extent of the problem
- Each partner's opinions regarding the problem
- The negative aspects of the problem
- The positive aspects of the problem

- How you both feel handling the problem in this way
- Alternative options in finding solutions to the problem
- How you would be affected if the problem remained unsolved
- Your perception and intuition regarding the problem
- Decide on the route you have jointly agreed upon in solving the problem and implement it
- Decide to review the agreement (give yourselves ample time to try alternative ways of handling and solving problems)

There may be thoughts and behaviors you should get rid of when dealing with problems.

Things to Banish

- Self-destructive thoughts and feelings
- Feelings of guilt and remorse
- Withdrawal from your partner
- Criticizing your partner
- Blaming your partner
- Repeating bad patterns and habits

There are many more things that can be added to all these lists that are unique to each of us.

> Most people are other people. Their thoughts are someone else's opinions, their lives a mimicry, their passions a quotation.
>
> Oscar Wilde

7 Letting Go of Your Unwanted Jealousy Baggage

This is a hard thing to do. Everyone brings unwanted baggage to a new relationship. It's perfectly normal. It is, however, damaging and unhealthy to bring negative destructive baggage into a relationship. Unwanted baggage is like a big black shadow constantly looming over you. You will see it in unlikely places and it can lead to intimidating, uncontrollable anger and violence. Some people will not accept that they have unwanted baggage; this usually leads to emotionally disconnected people who will find blame in everyone except themselves.

Here are some examples of destructive baggage:

- Old worn out habits
- Bad thinking patterns
- Negative emotions ("I can't do anything right")
- Expectations too high (he/she will never meet my needs)
- Expectations too low ("I don't expect anything to come of this")
- No expectations ("It's pointless trying because it won't work out anyway")
- Using the words "blame" and "fault" (it is never *me* who is wrong)
- Bad emotional experiences from the past
- Bad physical experiences from the past

There is a host of unwanted baggage that you can bring into a relationship. Try not to do this as you will not be giving your new relationship a chance to move forward in a healthy emotional manner.

Goal Setting

So that you are both clear about where you have been and where you are now, it will be important to structure joint goals so that you can go forward without the baggage of jealousy drowning you both.

What are goals?

- Goals are broad and objectives are narrow
- Goals are general intentions and objectives are precise
- Goals are intangible and objectives are tangible
- Goals are abstract and objectives are concrete
- Goals can't be validated as is and objectives can be validated

A goal is an intention that you both would like to achieve in your marriage. For example, a goal might be "to spend more quality time with each other," thereby lessening the chance of one or other partner being jealous. The target you should set, in order to reach your goal, is to make time for each other by reducing your separate evenings out in a week, or to reassess your budget in order to accommodate this quality time together.

Objectives

An objective is a specific step, a milestone, which enables you to accomplish a goal. Setting objectives involves a continuous process of decision-making. Knowledge of yourself and your relationship is a vital starting point in setting objectives. Effective objectives are stretching but achievable. If it doesn't stretch you to achieve it, it's probably trivial or not worth doing.[1]

S.M.A.R.T. Objectives

- Specific: are you both clear about what you want to achieve?
- Measurable: do you understand how to reach your objective?
- Attainable: can you both achieve this?
- Relevant: is this option the most appropriate?
- Time bound: can this be done in the time span you have allotted?

What are your objectives?

Example: You have been through a difficult time in your relationship and identified the triggers that set off jealousy, and you are now in a position to identify where you want your relationship to be in 6 months' time. You could say, "We want our relationship to include better communication, more honesty and trust, joint ventures, achievable aims, positive thinking habits, etc." You can add more according to your individual wants and needs.

Setting boundaries in your relationship:

In restructuring your relationship, it is important to identify first of all that the original structure of your relationship was not working for either of you. The jealousy that existed in your relationship made you both unhappy and divided/isolated you from each other. Relationships are fragile at the best of times, beware that jealousy can destroy the foundation your life was based on.

When one partner sets a course away from the other, one of you will end up feeling unhappy and unfulfilled. Your re-

---

[1] *Understanding Objectives.* San Diego State University. 2006

lationship must be managed by both of you. If you were in a business partnership for instance, you wouldn't permit that business relationship to become out of control, over-spent, over committed, would you? The same principle should be applied in personal relationships.

You should put into place an invisible boundary line in your relationship. Within this invisible line, you can both confidently place your joint emotional, physical, and financial secrets that are for you only to know; you can also place your trust in each other and in your relationship. You should both learn to manage your lives within this boundary. Inside your boundaries are the intimate foundations of your relationship. These are the things that bind you to each other. When this line is in place, both partners feel respected and loved and certainly not taken for granted.

When this boundary line is broken by one partner behaving/acting in a disrespectful manner, the other will feel abused and the boundary line will cease to function. When one partner's actions cause the other to feel humiliated, shamed, ignored, etc., then the partner who feels all these things is faced with defending themselves. Learning to defend yourself from your partner should not be an issue in a personal relationship. This is not how a healthy relationship should be. Discuss these issues with your partner in order for you to both understand your different views of your relationship and your understanding of boundaries in your relationship.

> When one door of happiness closes, another opens; but often we look so long at the closed door that we do not see the one which has opened for us.
>
> Helen Keller

8 | Emotional Happiness After Jealousy

Emotional happiness is what every couple strives to achieve. Many couples are successful in achieving emotional happiness and this is particularly so when a couple has worked through the issue of jealousy in their relationship. Unfortunately, your early learning experiences and role modeling might suggest that your happiness is in the hands of other people. This is wrong. You are responsible for creating your own happiness.

How many times have you heard someone say, "I don't know what I would do without my partner?" Thereby, they imply that without their partner, they are nothing. This is a false belief, which comes from their early learning experiences. If you have always believed that it is the responsibility of someone else to make you happy, then you have never tried to make yourself happy other than the task of finding a partner to do this for you.

Many marriages/partnerships stay together because one or both partners are afraid of being alone. In order to "stay the same" in a relationship, a person who is afraid of being alone will change their behavior in order to be the perfect person that they believe their partner wants. Taking this behavior to its ultimate conclusion, there is no wonder that this person would come to the point of being jealous as they have no self-respect and no self-worth.

This person will avoid being rejected by their partner by:

- Being submissive or servile;
- Being non-argumentative, a "yes" person;
- Being helpless (a victim);

- Being overly generous;
- Compromising their standards and principles;

Maybe you can add to this list. A person who has been or is behaving in this way has done this for so long that it has become a normal way to react. It's as if you are wearing a plastic mask and are behaving in an "unreal" way. By doing this, you are denying to yourself who you really are and what you really want. You have, unconsciously or consciously, hidden many aspects of your personality in order to keep your partner and accommodate to their needs and demands.

I will admit that I have been an expert at behaving in this way. I know because I remember consciously putting myself down, in order to ensure that my partner believed that I was far less than he was. I did this to make him feel that he had the power and control over me and my children. I believed this would stop him from leaving me. I had no self-belief, no self-worth, and the confidence I had was an "acting performance" from start to finish. I believed that if I behaved as "me" I would be disliked, unpopular, and rejected by my partner. I too was jealous during this period in my life, as I thought that every other woman was much better than I was. It has taken me many years and I have lived through unhappy emotional experiences before realizing and believing that I can be me because I am OK as I am.

Emotional happiness with a partner is a goal to aspire to. In our everyday environment, reading newspapers, watching television, reading magazines, etc., we are led to believe that there are many ways you can achieve happiness.

How to achieve happiness, according to popular media:
- Having possessions;
- Being successful in your chosen career;
- Wearing designer clothes;
- Living in a beautiful house;

- Being of slim build;
- Taking drugs (illegal substances);
- Acquiring the "right" type of friends;
- Being in the right social circles;
- Driving a flash car;

Do any of these things make you happy? They are just superficial things that are irrelevant to a happy, contented, loving, secure existence. No, owning stuff and acquiring the right kind of people around you does not make for long-term happiness. None of these things makes you happy. However, they can lead you to become jealous of other people's stuff.

The Only Things That Make You Really Happy

- Learning to like yourself just as you are and just as you aren't;
- Having personal satisfaction and achievements;
- The ability to accept someone else's opinion on an issue without having a "hissy fit";
- Being in an emotionally healthy relationship;
- Honest communication with a partner, your family, and friends;
- Learning to trust your partner;

Ultimately, happiness depends upon:

- How you choose to live your life
- The standards you live by
- Your personal integrity
- Your honesty with yourself
- Learning to be content with what you have

Attaining Emotional Happiness

What is emotional happiness?

- Making time for your relationship;
- Engaging in an honest relationship without guilty over-tones;
- When you can stop overreacting;
- Being able to work together and talk to each other if ei-ther of you is jealous;
- Living with positive values, moral codes, and ethics;
- When your partner is your best friend;
- Having a joint set of goals;
- Having faith in each other;
- Trusting each other;
- Remembering that if you don't want people stepping on you, don't act like a doormat;
- Remembering that what goes around comes around;
- Treating others as you want to be treated;
- Giving up the need to defend your point of view;
- Living in the present moment;
- Learning the three "Rs" — Respect for self, Respect for others, Responsibility for your actions;

As you overcome your jealousy issues, you will become more self-aware. The reason you are becoming more self-aware is that you have completed exercises I have suggested in this book that have forced you to look at your core be-liefs/habits/patterns and you have taken the necessary steps to address all these factors. When you experience jealousy, fear, anger, hostility, or resentment, you are in a state of emo-tional turmoil. The great challenge is to master these unwanted, difficult core-emotions and in their place create love, acceptance, respect, and emotional happiness. By con-tinuing to be self-aware, you can consciously choose to change your core-beliefs and change the way you interact with your partner and other people.

> "When guilt rears its ugly head, confront it, discuss it, and let it go. The past is over. ... Forgive yourself and move on."
>
> Bernie S. Siegel

Believe that you can...

- Have the power to change and be able to consolidate your thoughts, speech and action;
- Maintain the shift from your jealous tendencies so that you can communicate to your partner and other people with respect;
- Stop reacting in a jealous, emotional manner;
- Develop loving relationships based on respect;

Common Traits of Happy People

- Good self-esteem;
- Hopeful for the future;
- Confidence in themselves;
- Believe they are competent;
- Have staying power in living through the bad times;
- In control of themselves;
- Believe that they are definitely not a victim;
- Adaptable and flexible;
- A sense of well-being;
- A positive outlook on life;

Your old emotional core-belief system is embedded in your mind as a result of observing and copying your role-models during your childhood through learned behavior. You react to difficulties in the "here and now" just the same as you did in the "there and then." It's only when unsolvable problems arise in a relationship that you realize that you are repeating the same old stuff you have always believed and said having, but which has had no previous success.

You come to the point of changing your beliefs, usually through desperation after having tried every other method of understanding and communicating in your personal relationship with your partner. Most people get to this point and try to embrace the system I have identified as a last resort, having nothing else to try.

You will learn that if you do not live by your old core-belief system, you will no longer experience the devastating jealous reactions that you have clung to. You have lived on an emotional rollercoaster and have experienced a turbulent ride throughout your life. You are now in the process of climbing off the rollercoaster and are no longer a "victim" of the bad ride. You have the power over yourself. No one else has that power unless you give it to them.

You have the power to believe or disbelieve what your mind is telling you. Use that power positively and see through the bad habit and stop it in its tracks. When you change the way you express yourself, your partner will change the way she/he responds to you. With practice, you will be able to do this easily. Developing personal power enables you to recover from your usual self-destructive patterns and establish new, creative, and innovative ones.

I have been asked many times, how you can become happy after experiencing jealousy in your relationship. You might be depressed, pessimistic, unable to communicate, anxious, etc. Not everyone is born with good self-esteem, good self-worth, good self-confidence, an optimistic outlook. These people are, however, displaying bad repeating patterns that are filled with hopelessness and negativity. They are locked into a bad habit. One simple method of becoming a happy person is to act happy. "Act happy and you will become happy." Practice looking happy. If you do this, happy people will be attracted to you and, before very long, you will realize that you are actually happy. To be confident, act confident. Smile when you don't feel like smiling. In practicing this simple exercise, you are turning your negative traits into positive ones, and you will soon acquire the good habit of being happy. Happy people have control over their own lives. They are not puppets whose strings are pulled by their partners. People who have no control of themselves are vulnerable, helpless victims.

Learn to take the initiative in a discussion. Dare to say what you want. Stand up and be counted. Doing all these things will give you back your self-respect.

Other things to learn to do:
- Embrace change;
- Let jealous thoughts go;
- Build upon change;
- Be courageous;
- Become the person you want to be;
- Accept that you cannot change your partner;
- Accept personal responsibility and accountability;
- Treat yourself with kindness, caring, and compassion;
- Be non-judgmental of self;
- Take care of your loving partnership;
- Treat others as you want to be treated (remember the law of karma);
- Be grateful for what you have rather than focusing on what you don't have;
- Laugh with your partner;
- Spend time with your partner;
- Do things together;
- Find out what your fears are and overcome them;

This is a long list. Why not turn it into your joint personal goals? After the discomfort of feeling jealous, your relationship will only get better if you are both prepared to build a solid, honest foundation in your relationship. Inside the front cover of Daniel Goleman's book, *Emotional Intelligence* it says,

> "Emotional Intelligence includes self-awareness and impulse control, persistence, zeal and self-motivation, empathy and social deftness. These are the hallmarks of character and self-discipline, of altruism and compassion – basic capabilities needed if our society is to thrive."

Some ways to stay happy in a relationship:

- Your reactions to your partner should remain the same whether you are two months, two years, or 22 years into to your relationship;
- Hug ("cwtch" a Welsh Word meaning hugging) and kiss your partner on a regular basis (you are never too old to hug and kiss);
- You should trust each other. There is no short-cut to trusting your partner apart from believing in your own perception of them. Trust should not be given automatically. It should be allowed to build up and develop over the weeks, months, years in your relationship;
- Trust yourself. Don't cheat, don't lie, don't gossip;
- Praise your partner for his/her efforts in your relationship;
- Focus on the positive aspects of your relationship and undo the negative aspects;
- Never verbally or physically attack your partner. Instead, choose to remain calm and negotiate with your partner for a compromise.

> "The only way to avoid being miserable is not to have enough leisure to wonder whether you are happy or not."
>
> George Bernard Shaw

9 | Living the Dream After Jealousy

A healthy, happy relationship

What makes a healthy, happy relationship? Here are some examples:

- Having trust in each other;
- Feeling safe and secure together;
- Being able to share thoughts and feelings with each other without recriminations;
- Being mutually respectful;
- Having fun and laughing together;

Each relationship is unique, and the elements of the relationship that confirm to you both that you are happy may be different from the above examples. A healthy relationship stays that way with continued effort by both partners working to keep it healthy. In my experience, the minute you allow yourself to slip into a comfort zone is when things can go wrong between the two of you. Make sure you stay alert in order to offset this happening.

Suggestions for keeping the relationship healthy:

- Both of you making a commitment to be honest with each other;
- Both of you understanding that you are both unique individuals with different thoughts, feelings, and interests on some issues. Accept this and listen to what your partner is saying. Treat it as is important;
- Both of you being able to give your point of view over an issue and compromising on the outcome;

- By learning that sometimes you have to agree to disagree and find a common route that both partners will accept;

- By giving each other space to develop on a personal level;

- By celebrating your differences;

- By enjoying hobbies/projects together;

- By knowing and understanding that you will have disagreements and rows in the future, but instead of this situation causing a major disruption, you will both manage the disagreement in a calm, organized way, allowing both partners to discuss, at length if necessary, their viewpoint ;

- By accepting that sometimes you will be wrong during discussions, and learning how to handle this situation in a mature way.

Romantic Marriage/Business Partnership

A theory I have subscribed to defines marriage much the same as you would a business partnership agreement. The skills you use in the workplace can work just as effectively in your relationship and in your home.

Ask yourself, "How would the ideal employee react at work?" How is this different from the way you react at home?

- At work, you learn quickly that jealousy will not be tolerated;

- At work, you are almost always alert to the different changes that occur;

- At work, you ensure that your work colleagues know immediately there is a change in policy at your organization;

- At work, you make a habit of thinking before opening your mouth to speak;
- At work, your communication with others is clear so as to avoid misinterpretation;
- At work, you are even tempered and do not fly off the handle;
- At work, you want to be liked and respected;
- At work, you are helpful to your colleagues and they are, in turn, helpful to you;
- At work, you get praise and are rewarded when you overcome a difficult obstacle;
- At work, you are enthusiastic and driven in order to step up the ladder;
- At work, you will sit and listen to a lot of rubbish being talked about but you do not and would not be rude and dismissive;
- At work, everyone knows their individual job description and it governs the way they work;
- At work, you know the administrative process and stick to the rules;
- At work, you show respect to your colleagues;
- At work, you use problem-solving skills;
- At work, you set realistic goals.

As you move on from experiencing pangs of jealousy and behaving in a jealous manner, you must understand that you will still have to deal with conflicts with your partner. During these times, it is vital that you do not bring the jealousy habit back into the relationship during these difficult times.

Overcoming Conflict

Here are some examples/tips for overcoming conflict:
- Remember to be very clear about the issue;

- Remember to listen keenly to what your partner is saying;
- Resist the temptation to drag up old arguments and disagreements;
- Resist swearing and calling your partner names;
- Don't enter into a disagreement when either of you are drunk;
- Do so when you are both alone at home (children in bed). Don't be tempted to bite back while visiting other people, for example;
- Don't avoid the issue by diverting the conversation or agreeing with your partner for the sake of peace and quiet;
- Stop using words like "fault" and "blame";
- Remember to search for the middle ground;
- Always admit and take personal responsibility for your part in the disagreement;

Conflict occurs in all relationships. It is a normal part of a relationship of two independent individuals living with each other and sharing their time together. It is, therefore, very important to know how to deal with the conflicts when they arise. It is important to stay calm, level-headed, and honest about what you say and how you feel. The more you practice this interaction between the two of you, the easier it will get. Always be aware of dredging up your jealous, resentful, destructive remarks that you did prior to learning a new way forward.

Rules for conflict:

- Don't try to catch each other out in an argument. No slyly creeping up on your partner when he/she least expects you;
- Organize your thoughts;

- Know what you want and why you want it;
- Know what you are going to say and be clear when you speak;
- Listen to your partner when he/she speaks;
- Don't interrupt each other;
- Stick to the point; don't divert and bring other stuff up. It will only confuse you;
- When your partner makes a point, repeat it to him/her (paraphrasing) to assure him/her and to make sure that you have understood this point;
- You should not apportion blame on each other;
- Don't dredge up past arguments;
- Compromise and negotiate;
- Don't raise your voice or be aggressive;
- Don't deliberately hurt each other with spontaneous harsh words;
- Don't overreact;
- Stay calm;
- Avoid hidden agendas;
- When issues can't be resolved, leave them for another day and time. Don't force a conclusion on the issue in hand;
- When you have made a decision, choose who is going to take the lead and give a time span to allow the task to be achieved;
- Don't be afraid to return to the discussion at a later date and say that the task didn't work out as you'd both planned. Sometimes you have to try several options before hitting on the right course of action.

"Peace comes not from the absence of conflict, but from the ability to cope with it."

— Anonymous

10 | The Emotional Journey After Jealousy

James 3:16 says, "For where jealousy and selfish ambition exist, there is disorder and every evil thing" (NAS). Congratulations, you have arrived at the final step in this book. Let's look back and see how far you have come.

You have had the opportunity of learning...

- That overcoming jealousy is a constant challenge
- That jealousy comes from habit-forming early negative thought patterns
- How to get rid of your early negative thought patterns and replace them with positive thought patterns
- To let resentment and bitterness go
- To trust
- To think before you speak
- Personal and shared responsibility
- Personal and shared accountability
- How to communicate with your partner
- How to resolve conflict
- The importance of mutual respect
- The importance of joint financial responsibility
- How to compromise
- How to talk and act without behaving in a threatening manner
- What qualities and characteristics are important in a partner
- Your must-haves and your have-nots in your relationship

- To be comfortable with each other

These are only some examples of the opportunities you have had by reading this book. Some of you reading this book might have already given up on trying to work through your jealous emotion. Some of you might still be blaming your partner for their indiscretion and feel unable to look at your part in the betrayal that has occurred. If this is true for you, then you have to ask yourself "what next?"

Why do you refuse to look within and work through the process?

- Perhaps you are too frightened of what you will find out about yourself;
- Perhaps you are scared of remembering your child-hood;
- Perhaps it's because you know that you have been gul-lible and foolish in trusting your partner;
- Perhaps you don't think your relationship is worth sav-ing;
- Perhaps you have discovered your partner cheating many times and have not given up all hope of ever changing the status quo;
- Perhaps you feel you cannot change;
- Perhaps it's because you feel strongly that you shouldn't have to change and believe that your partner is the one who should be changing;
- Perhaps it's because you are tired, depressed, lethargic, anxious, stressed, or panicky;
- Perhaps it's because now is not the right time for you to do this;
- Perhaps the first step to take is to prepare your mind to accept the thought of tackling this issue soon;

Not everyone can move through the process of jealousy and emerge recovered from the trauma they have experienced. If this is the case for you, then the jealousy will eventually rot the relationship from the inside out. Some people go through life believing they are not jealous, envious, or unhappy. They stay in the cocoon they have made for themselves that feels comfortable. To change your thoughts, feelings, and reactions is a risky business and has to be attempted with some reserve and caution. If you are the jealous person, you will have a resource of thoughts, emotions, and reactions within you that you will turn to that will make you believe that you are right in your assumptions and these resources are designed to permit you to "stay as you are."

Life is not straightforward. It's not black and white. Life happens in the gray areas. To feel good about your relationship, you must feel good about yourself first. In order to feel good, you have to face all your fears and deal with each of them. Allow yourself time to do this, but please start doing this now.

Fears in Communicating With Your Partner

A jealous partner will find it difficult to share personal feelings with his/her partner, due to fear of sounding childish, paranoid, and stupid. The partner who is on the receiving end of jealousy will be afraid to be honest in communicating just in case something innocently said is taken the wrong way by the jealous partner.

Fears you may find difficult to share with your partner:
- Fear of being rejected by my partner
- Fear that my partner will think I am weak
- Fear of looking like a fool
- Fear that I will be laughed at
- Fear of revealing too much information about me

- Fear that my partner will blame me
- Fear that my partner will not accept his/her part in the situation
- Fear of being too truthful
- Fear that my partner will not understand what I am trying to say
- Fear that my partner is not interested in what I say
- Fear of not being taken seriously
- Fear that my partner will see me as too complicated and difficult to live with

The above examples are the natural thoughts of people who are scared of revealing themselves to their partner. These people have lived, for many years in some cases, believing that if they revealed who they really are and what thoughts they have, then their partner will reject them.

> "We need people in our lives with whom we can be as open as possible. To have real conversation with people may seem like such a simple, obvious suggestion, but it involves courage and risk."
>
> — Thomas Moore

Learn To Love Each Other

Here are some examples of how to show you love your partner:

- Don't go to sleep on a quarrel;
- Show your partner that he/she is appreciated by you;
- Don't mind the little trivial things. Look past the small insignificant stuff;
- Show affection on a regular basis;
- Keep your intimate relationship alive and exciting;

- Don't take your problems out on your partner. If you have had a bad day, toss it aside before your partner comes home;

- Don't try to change your partner—remember you can only change yourself;

- Don't keep secrets from each other;

- Remember birthdays, anniversaries, etc.;

- Remember when you didn't need TV to occupy your thoughts, and turn it off sometimes and just chat;

"To be, or not to be--that is the question"

Of course, this is a quote from William Shakespeare's play *Hamlet,* written some 400 years ago. However, this sentence can apply to anything in the modern world. To be happy or to be unhappy? Ask yourself, "Do I want to be happy?" If this answer is "no," I believe it is safe to say that your life is already programmed to continued misery. If you answer "yes," you can make the decision here and now to become happy. Love, success, happiness are a choice you can make and achieve. None of these basic desires are yours by right; you have to find them. Nothing comes for free in this life. You have to strive and work hard for what you want.

The first thing to do, if you want to be happy, is to become happy *inside* yourself. Be happy with yourself first and see how your relationships and your view of life change as a result of this. If you are happy inside, you will be positive and confident in what you are doing, where you are going, who you are going with. Nothing will make you truly happy unless you have found inner happiness.

Happy is also a feeling you get when things go right for you. Is this true happiness? I think not, otherwise everything and everyone you become involved with would have to succeed in order for you to continue being happy. The purchase of jewels, houses, cars, holidays are the things you can buy that give you temporary pleasure, but they do not, and will not, provide you with inner peace and contentment or long-term happiness. Having a relationship with someone special, however, will give you long-term pleasure and that is something that money can't buy.

> "The greatest danger for most of us is not that our aim is too high and we miss it, but that it is too low and we reach it."
>
> — Michelangelo

Through this book, I have taken you through the journey of jealousy and how it can impact on your relationship. I have also given you some suggestions, options, and ideas on how to rid yourself of jealousy from your relationship or, at least, how to counteract it. Having a good relationship depends on how much work you are both prepared to put into it to make it what you both want it to be. Many of you search for happiness through someone else. This is because you don't believe that you can be happy with your own resources. In order to be complete, you have to find the source of inner contentment and happiness that is available for everyone.

I can hear you saying that "I want to be happy, but it is my circumstances that make me unhappy, and this has nothing to do with me." How can you change this situation? You can change your unhappy state of mind by changing the negative forces that have put you in a place of unhappiness. Try surrounding yourself with people who are positive; people who embrace change; people who are not afraid to look at themselves; people who never give up; people who see the glass as half full (positive) not half empty (negative). Every situation and circumstance you find yourself in can be interpreted two ways, happy-unhappy (positive-negative). Happiness isn't about how much money you have, it's more about your belief system, your thought processes, and your attitude to yourself, your partner, and other people who are close to you.

Unhappiness Has Its Benefits

If you feel you are thwarted in life because you seem depressed, insecure, self-doubting, and with a low self-esteem, then I can guarantee that you will be the focus of negative attention by your partner, family, and friends who want you to be happy. In other words, there are rewards for being unhappy.

Here are some examples of the negative rewards you will get:

- You will get more negative attention from your partner, family, and friends;
- You will get more negative reactions from your partner, family, and friends;
- You will be left out of being involved in the decision process of any discussion, because you believe you are unable to contribute (another way of opting out of responsibility) and those people close to you will come to believe this also;
- You may not be expected to work for a living;
- You will be excused from doing some or all domestic chores;

There are many more that you can identify in your own life. If you feel any of the above, then you will be powerless to achieve any of your needs, wants, and desires. You will have no passion, enthusiasm, or drive to accomplish anything, believing that you can't do it! Emotional pain is as damaging as any physical pain you can experience. Emotional pain will gain your attention over everything, ensuring that you stay in the emotionally painful rut you are in.

If you project an image of being happy, you will...

- Be more successful in your career;
- Be liked and more popular;
- Get positive support from your partner, family, and friends;
- Have a much improved relationship with your partner;
- Have confidence, self-respect, and a feeling of self-worth;
- Be better equipped to deal with difficult situations;
- Have more control of your life;
- Be optimistic;

These are only some of the many benefits to being happy. Happiness is the "bread and water" of life and as such it provides you with the drive, enthusiasm, and passion to do whatever it is you want to achieve.

Health, happiness, and love surely have to be what most people say they want in their lives. You can spend your whole life searching for "the one" and never find this person. Experience has taught me that the only way to connect to someone with a healthy belief system is to have a healthy belief system yourself. If you fail to do so, you will automatically link to people who are negative, with unhealthy belief systems that will erode the relationship in due course.

You cannot and should not look to find a partner in order to make you whole. No one should have that much responsibility placed on their shoulders. A relationship that survives and moves on after experiencing the destructive emotion of jealousy is a better relationship than before the situation occurred. You have had the opportunity of really looking at yourself and each other. To be able to open yourself out to your partner is very difficult for most people. No one wants to feel vulnerable. No one wants to give their partner open access to the things that hurt, destroy, humiliate, and puncture their soul.

It takes two committed, courageous people to proceed through this journey of discovery and arrive at the end with their emotions intact. The fact is that by going through this experience, you can and should recover from the process, feeling confident, able with self-respect and self-worth that you know will stand you in good stead in your future together.

"Paradoxical Commandments"
By Kent M. Keith

People are often unreasonable, illogical, and self-centered;
Forgive them anyway.

If you are kind, people may accuse you of selfish, ulterior motives;
Be kind anyway.

If you are successful, you will win some false friends and some true enemies. If you are honest and frank, people may cheat you;
Be honest and frank anyway.

What you spend years building, someone could destroy overnight;
Build anyway.

If you find serenity and happiness, they may be jealous;
Be happy anyway.

The good you do today, people will often forget tomorrow;
Do good anyway.

Give the world the best you have, and it may never be enough;
Give the world the best you've got anyway.

You see, in the final analysis, it is between you and GOD. It was never between you and them anyway.

Reportedly seen hung on a wall in one of Mother Theresa's orphanages.

Appendix A: Emergency Contacts

International Contacts:

1-800-THERAPIST (1-800-843-7274)	1-800-843-7274
Find-a-Therapist.com	1.866.450.3463
POWA Helpline	(011) 642-4345
The American Domestic Violence Crisis Line	866-USWOMEN

In Canada:

Assaulted Women's Helpline	416-863-0511
Domestic Violence Hotline	1-800-799-7233
National Domestic Violence Hotline	1-800-363-9010

In Australia:

Domestic Violence Crisis Hotline (NSW)	1800 656 463
Domestic Violence Crisis Hotline (Northern Territory)	1800 019 116
Domestic Violence Crisis Hotline (Queensland)	1800 811 811
Domestic Violence Crisis Hotline (South Australia)	1800 800 098
Domestic Violence Crisis Hotline (Tasmania)	1800 633 937
Domestic Violence Crisis Hotline (Victoria)	1800 007 339

In the United Kingdom:

Action on Elder Abuse Hotline	0808 808 8141
Muslim Women's Help Line	0181 904 8193
National Domestic Violence Hotline	0808 2000 247
Northern Ireland Women's Aid Federation	(028) 90 331818

In the United States:

Asian Task Force against Domestic Violence Hotline	617-338-2355
Crisis Support Network	1-800-435-7276
National Domestic Violence Hotline	1-800-799-7233
Safe Horizon's Domestic Violence Hotline	800-621-4673
The American Domestic Violence Crisis Line	1-866-USWOMEN
The National Coalition Against Domestic Violence	303-839-1852

Bibliography

Amen, D. G. (1998). *Change your brain, change your life: The breakthrough program for conquering anxiety, depression, obsessiveness, anger, and impulsiveness.* New York: Times Books.

Brady, T. (2007). *Regaining control: When love becomes a prison.* Ann Arbor, MI: Loving Healing Press.

Covey, S. (1990). *The 7 habits of highly effective people.* A fireside book. New York: Simon & Schuster.

Davies, L. (1992) *Allies in healing: When the person you love was sexually abused as a child.* San Francisco: Harper Perennial

Goleman, D. (1995). *Emotional intelligence.* New York: Bantam Books.

Gray, J. (1998) *Men are from Mars, Women are from Venus.* Harper Collins

Jeffers, S. J. (1996). *End the struggle and dance with life: How to build yourself up when the world gets you down.* New York: St. Martin's Press.

Jeffers, S. (1997). *Feel the fear and do it anyway: How to turn your fear and indecision into confidence and action.* London: Rider.

Keith, K. M. (2002). *Anyway: The paradoxical commandments: finding personal meaning in a crazy world.* New York: Putnam.

Lew, M. (1990). *Victims no longer: Men recovering from incest and other sexual child abuse.* New York: Perennial Library.

McKenna, P., & Willbourn, H. (2006). *I can mend your broken heart.* London: Bantam.

Murphy, J. G. (2005). *Getting even: Forgiveness and its limits.* New York: Oxford University Press.

Norwood, R. (1985). *Women who love too much: When you keep wishing and hoping he'll change*. Los Angeles: J.P. Tarcher.

Norwood, R. (1994). *Why me, why this, why now: A guide to answering life's toughest questions*. New York: C. Southern Books

Pease, B., & Pease, A. (2000). *Why men don't listen & women can't read maps: How we're different and what to do about it*. New York, NY: Welcome Rain

Randall, P. (2001). *Bullying in adulthood: Assessing the bullies and their victims*. New York: Brunner-Routledge.

Volkman, M. (2005) *Life Skills: Improve the Quality of Your Life with Metapsychology*. Loving Healing Press: Ann Arbor, MI.

About the Author

Lynda Bevan lives in a picturesque village in South Wales, United Kingdom. She is 59 years of age, married for the third time, with three (adult) children. During her teens and early twenties, she pursued and enjoyed acting and taught drama at local Youth Centers.

Her 22-year career has involved working in the area of mental health, with the two major care agencies in the UK, Social Services and the National Health Service.

After the birth of her third child, and with her second marriage ending, she became employed by Social Services and climbed through the ranks to senior management level with some speed.

During her career with Social Services, she developed a passion for counseling and psychotherapy and worked extensively with mental health patients within the organization, setting up counseling projects in Healthcare Centers. The task was to tackle the issue of doctors who inappropriately referred patients to Psychiatric Hospitals for therapy when they had experienced events that arise in normal everyday life, e.g., divorce, anxiety, depression, bereavement, stress, loss of role. It was during this time that she became involved in marital/relationship counseling and, coincidentally, was experiencing difficulties within her own relationship. The experience of working in this environment, and her own relationship issues, enabled Lynda to be innovative; creating methods of coping and developing strategies that enabled her and her patients to live within their problematic relationships. These strategies were devised and offered to patients who had clearly identified that they did not want to separate or proceed with the divorce process.

After taking early retirement from Social Services, she became employed by the National Health Service as a Counselor in the Primary Healthcare Setting. During this period in her career, she began using the strategies she had developed with patients who were referred for relationship counseling and who did not want to end their partnership/marriage. These strategies have been used extensively over a ten-year period with impressive results.

Lynda is presently employed as a Manager of a charity that supports people who are HIV positive. She is also the Resident Relationship Counselor on Swansea Sound Radio.

Index

Exclusive offer for readers of *Life Without Jealousy!*

Order Form – 15% Discount Off List Price!

Ship To:

☐ **VISA**   ☐ **MasterCard**   ☐ check to
Loving Healing Press

_____
Name

_____   _____ _____/_____
Address   Card #   Expires

_____
Address   _____
                                                                           Signature

_____ _____   Life Skills   ____ x $14.50 = _____
City   State

                                                              Lover Walks Out _____ x $13 = _____
_____ _____ _____
District   Country   Zip/Post code   Life After Betrayal ____ x $13 = _____

_____   Subtotal = _____
Daytime phone #

                                                              Michigan Residents: 6% tax = _____
_____
email address   Shipping charge (see below)   _____

                                                              Your Total _$_____

Shipping price <u>per copy</u> via:
☐ Priority Mail (+ $3.50) ☐ Int'l Airmail (+ $4) ☐ USA MediaMail/4th Class (+ $2)

Fax Order Form back to (734)663-6861 or
Mail to LHP, 5145 Pontiac Trail, Ann Arbor, MI 48105

LaVergne, TN USA
19 January 2010
170566LV00003B/94/P